The Sacred Two

the She and He of Creation...

by

Mary Saint-Marie/Sheoekah

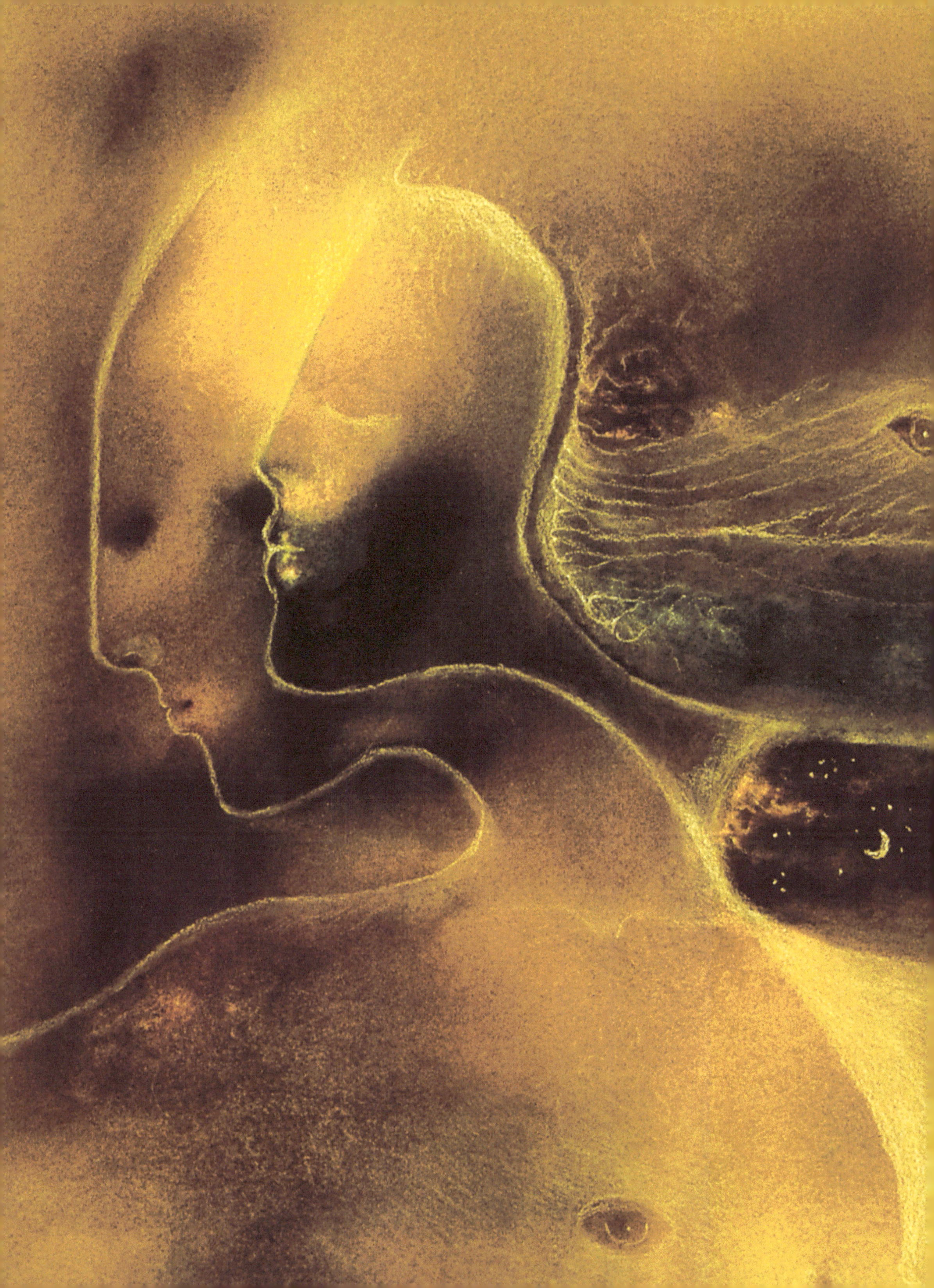

THE SACRED TWO

the SHE and HE of Creation...

...an invitation to the Wedding...
of the ONE manifest
as the Star-Stone Two

Mary Saint-Marie
Sheoekah

Second Edition, Revised 2015

Published by Ancient Beauty Studio, www.marysaintmarie.com

ISBN: 978-0964657281 (sc)

All artwork by Mary Saint-Marie

Cover Art: *and together...they dream and sing...*

Titlepage Art: *Ancient Beauty He and She*

This book is dedicated to
the dance of the ONE as The Sacred Two
in all of Creation...

and to those who are already living
Spirit-ordained unions...

Cover Art and Poem by Mary Saint-Marie

and together...they dream and sing...

and together...they dream

and sing of worlds unseen...

and together...they build...

the royal twos...they build...

and the tribes...they land...

in the sacred two by twos...

they know well...

and they remember...

Imaged here is the Unmanifest One, manifest as The Sacred Two.
Imaged here is the sacredness of that holy union.

Let me say that when I speak of
The Sacred Two that I speak of the One.
There is no other.

These are the words that came to me
from the Silence one dawn,
after I had begun compiling the
passages of this book.

It seems so simple.

The undivided and unmanifest ONE

appears as the divided and manifest…TWO

ever longing to reunite

as

The Sacred Two

The Sacred Two, man and woman,
balanced and equal, is the basis of an enduring culture.

It is the Dance of the ONE manifest.

It is pure science manifest.

IT is pure poetry manifest.

It is inviolate.

It is inexorable.

It is the natural Law of Balance.

It is the Yin and the Yang.

It is peace manifest.

It is love manifest.

And, war, it is no more.

Contents

Passages of The Sacred Two

Poetry of SHE and HE

Acknowledgments

I deeply thank my precious daughters, Kimberly and Rebecca, for just being in my life. At times I felt like a balloon with two strings, one for each of them, and that their walks by my side provided unspeakable grace. They have watched me follow this illumined thread of The Sacred Two in many forms and in all my human ups and downs.

I thank Laura Daen for the gift of creative and sacred friendship as this book coalesced.

Immense gratitude goes forth to all of The Sacred Two relationships...which I began to meet in the eighties and nineties. Your lives and presence brighten the planet; you reflect such balance inwardly and outwardly to all you meet. Your stories are needed.

And appreciation fills my heart for all the ones I have worked with in Soul Sessions/ Retreats and Initiations into the Ancient Yin/Yang Circle. Your receptivity and openness to the Holy Presence brings such insight to the enactment by the true partners.

Many years of grace have filled my life in the painting of commissioned paintings of The Sacred Two. Thank you all. Such universal insight came while painting and attuning; yet how simple and how natural.

I thank Aaron Rose for this second edition of *The Sacred Two.* Aaron's gift of attuning to the soul of books is an elevated contribution.

On the practical level of putting this book together, I thank the following:
Art scanning by Light Source Creations, Medford, Oregon.
Book design and revision by Aaron Rose, Mount Shasta, California.

I thank the host of inner and outer teachers
who have guided me to the ONE...inner Presence...
that I might have the visions and journeys to inner realms to share the book...

Introduction

The purpose of this oracle book, The Sacred Two, is to unveil the eternal Principle of Balance...of the One...manifest as HE and SHE...the yin and yang of all creation.

Presence...the ONE...unmanifest...undivided...formless...timeless...
manifest as the divided two...formed...timed...
The Sacred Two ever longing to reunite...
in man and woman...
in the kingdoms...
in the elements...
in all of nature...
and in all the processes of nature...

The purpose of revealing this principle is that it may be lived...demonstrated in our lives...your life, my life, the One Life that we are. That we may find revealed in our lives...the Mystical as the Practical. That we may find an application of this principle in everyday life. That we may experience the ordinary as extraordinary. That the seemingly mundane is known as the magical, the revelation of the mysteries.

We are It!
The Beholders of the Mystery...
The Beholders of the Infinite...unfolding as a flower...

Let us enter into this *Realm of the Real...*
the once upon a non-time.

Let us enter the Land of the Fairy Tales where all is possible now...

Let us enter into the world of *and they lived happily ever after...*
and the story begins...

Let us imagine...

Let us pretend...
as a child in the wonder of creation...
that the garden, the paradise, the elysian field...
is already here...

It is here in our consciousness that appears within
and in our Earth that appears without...

It is here...

There is no doubt that we may all look out unto the appearance world and see that on the physical plane of existence much seems impure and ignoble, lacking in beauty and grace.

For a moment...be aware...the Garden is here...the Garden is already here...

What a thought! Now in our poetic and visual odyssey, in our MAKE Believe...
let us Remember...

Remembering...
Remembering...
We are Remembering...
We are Remembering our part in the Garden...

The Garden...that is the Earth...is our playground, our sandpile, our stage where we act out love...the principle of Balance...the ONE as The Sacred Two. First individually, then with our partners and the kingdoms and the elements. And with our friends, our relatives, our ancestors...and even with our imagined enemies. It is a fairy tale full of wonder...with one man and one woman ever acting out "their search, their preparation, their coming together." This union. This holy marriage is part of our joy of being, part of the One as the Many.

This holy dance of opposites...first inner, then outer...in a ceremony of creator's dance of creation. This Dance of Creation is played out in the dance of man and woman in original love. And it may be found like a treasure over and yet over again in Nature in the exalted dance of the opposites, ever giving and regiving, as the sky does rain to the earth and the earth does regive the moisture from her seas and oceans to make again the clouds upon our sky. The container and the essence contained...acted out in Nature over and over and over...in endless and infinite epiphanies. Everywhere we are surrounded by the lovemaking of the dance of the lover and the beloved, The Sacred Two, the dance of opposites, the dance of the ONE.

Lovemaking...it is all the same!
A mountain pool receiving a fresh spring rain...drop upon drop...
A flower drinking in the rays of sun...
A fire consuming yet another branch...
A yoni open now to love...

We may see it everywhere...should we begin to look...should we begin to see. We live ever in an electrically sexed universe, and union, the orgasm of life, is everywhere present.

Even in the mechanics of construction we may see the dance of opposites...in the nut and the bolt...in the hammer/nail and the hole. It is everywhere about as we begin to perceive our world as the garden...the garden of the Dance of Opposites...the Dance of the One as The Sacred Two...the dance of the One as the many.

We then begin to see through the single eye...with new awareness...that nothing else is happening on this planet. This truly is the only act, the only dance. We may have ones yet living in separation from the Source, as yet unable to surrender, to be open and receptive, who are living out a distortion or a perversion of the dance. But truly, there is only One dance, One garden, One Presence.

And as we find that Oneness within, we may allow our part to emerge from the Universal Archetypal Realm of the Real where there is one original man and one original woman, the twin origins. From that sacred place, all jealousies, envies, misunderstandings, and games borne of fear, they shall fall away.

And Remembering...it does come...
We Remember...our dance...
Our part in the fairy tale...allows each day a beholding of the dance...
around us and as us.
Just imagine. Let the image in...

Just imagine that you are the temple of Infinity, the template of Infinity, the temple template of Infinity, singing your song of your soul at dawn...

I AM Infinity; play through me...

Imagine that ecstasy. Imagine knowing that nothing else is going on. Nothing else. What then, this day, will you do or create in this garden of the Infinite? What do you remember of Infinity? What is the expression of your individual template?

And no matter the size of your external garden. Your garden is in your consciousness. Your garden is within. The world is within. So begin where you are. Create on a little paper, on a square foot of soil, in your kitchen or a journal. The power is not in the size. The power is in the only place of power. The Power is in the Infinite. It never leaves there. It is never in the personal. It only appears as so. The glory...is the ONE Power...and is ever in Presence. Be willing to start where you are to express your Dance in the Garden.

Create a space, a sacred space…on paper, in soil, a song in space…wherever you are. Begin where you are! Be willing to do whatever it takes to understand how to create in the Garden. It is your altar of Life. This is sacred enactment from the inside out when life is seen as the Dance of the One, as the dance of the lover and beloved in all the relationships…

And then…the magic…it does continue…for the Dance of The Sacred Two, both within and without, sets a stage, a platform, an altar, a literal foundation for the Many as the One. When one has experienced the consciousness of Oneness, of union…then there is a feeling and knowing of the interconnectedness. It may happen differently for each of us. We are unique. We might experience our Oneness, our relatedness, first with the elements…of the earth and the water and fire and air. Or we may come into unity first with the kingdoms…a horse, a lotus, or a stone from beneath your foot. These are primal and shamanic mergings. One may sit at the water's edge and be the very waterfall, the very mist across the lips…

Or our experiences of Oneness might be more galactic, more multi-dimensional, as merging with a star, your soul group, or merging with the original archetypes or with the very sky and the very earth as one. Or you may behold your very body as the container of Infinity or see the paradox in consciousness of all that is outside of you is inside…a grand experience of expansion to behold. Or you might experience Galactic Shamanism…the merging of the opposites…the alchemy of the marriage of love and wisdom merged as the ineffable, the unspeakable, and even the unthinkable…and Beauty…it does come…

This circle of Oneness is the yin and yang. It is the One manifest as The Sacred Two. It began to be revealed to me in vision many years ago by White Buffalo Woman, Changing Woman, Spider Woman. The power of purity was revealed to me by the ancient circle of Blue Kachinas. The yang protection was unveiled by the procession of endless Native Chieftains who act as the alchemical holder of the vision of the Twos. And the gargoyle that is the mouth at the center of the Aztec calendar serves as the protector of the Vision of the Two by Twos of the new world.

Together…are we ever on this poetic odyssey.

It is mindless and timeless and emerges out of the blackest void. It is ecstatic.
It is indeed the dance of he and she…in endless forms.
Archetypal HE and SHE! We are the very myth.
Books and legends and great epics may inspire and remind us here and there.
But they cannot take us there.
We are the very myth.

We are the vessel through which this light may flow…
We are creator's dance…
We are the very place where the seeming inner and outer synapse.
Find that place. Feel it. Allow it.

Allow the Self to be moved, sounded, silenced, and stilled. Allow the Self to be. In that vast Silence comes the union, the alabaster marriage. Then…it is…that one is a conscious living vessel of Presence.

It is time to live our lives consciously connected to this presence of Light, with no intercessors, no mediators. The true teachers are educators, that is, they draw out in others what is already within. They inspire. That is true education.

Life is an invitation to The Dance…
Life is an invitation to the enactment of balance…
Life is the…as within…so without…
Life is the dance of Beauty…
Life is Living Ceremony…

This oracle book is shared to behold the dance…

Sacred, Ceremonial, and Inspired Use of the Oracle Book

This oracle book was designed to be used in whatever way one is inspired from within. There are fifty-two images and the fool. There are seventeen images of Archetypal-SHE, seventeen images of Archetypal-HE and seventeen images of The Sacred Two. And there is the Fool that may be used in any way one is guided.

Below are some of the ways that you may want to use this book:

Make contact with the Inner Presence, your very own Self. A meditation is offered at the end of the ideas below.

Create what to you is the perfect sacred ceremonial environment and mood and tone for the experience with the oracle book. Look inwardly and see what might add beauty and illumination and consciousness to each experience. Candles, visitors from the mineral kingdom, soft flowing clothing, perfect time of day or night, pillows, scents, gifts, invitation to those angelic ones in the realm of Enlightened Ones...and no distractions.

Or create your own new and unique ways of using the book individually or with your sacred partner or with groups.

One may experience some of the following ideas to come into deeper realization of the ONE as The Sacred Two. Enter the Realm of the Real and be the vessel of never ending illuminations. Be the vessel for "seeing" the birthing new world and beyond.

1. Ask a question or state a problem:

Ask a very lucid question or state simply a problem. Open the book to an image. Allow yourself to spontaneously be aware of the answer or the solution as you view the image and read the companion poem. Do not try to mentally get an answer. Do not try at all. Be empty and still and silent. Allow it. Know the image and/or poem may reflect what is Already within you to know or be. Trust.

2. Ask no question and state no problem:

Be in the consciousness beyond questions and problems. Now open the book to an image. Allow that image to have a voice, borne from your own Inner Knowing. Allow that image to commune intimately with you. Notice how simply an answer or an awareness may come from your Soul even when there is no question. You have opened to deeply feeling your inner Awareness. You are tapping Divine Intelligence that already knows.

3. For individual man or woman:

Choose three images from the book. Choose an image for your inner feminine. Choose an image for your inner masculine. And choose an image for your Inner Union, the Beloved. Allow each of these images to have a voice of wisdom, direct knowing from within. Allow your Soul to express what it feels and knows. (Let go of the human limited concept of "I don't know.")

Or choose three images for your outer HE, your outer SHE, and for the outer Sacred Two. Allow the inner Presence, your Beingness, to translate the images. Allow Soul translation to heighten and expand your awareness. Feel the rightness of inner knowingness.

4. For couples:

Be sure that both of you hold the book before you begin, so that the energies of both of you are part of the spontaneous ceremony that follows. Become aware of two questions or concerns. Each person may choose an image from the book. Go within and open to interpretations from your Inner Presence. Take turns sharing what you each receive from the visionary images and poems. Allow universal Soul to speak from in your heart. This sharing is an alchemical Cauldron of Communing. Allow this depth of communing of the Sacred Two. Feel your own soul. Feel the other's soul. Allow for great understanding and compassion and unconditional love. This becomes a sacred ceremonial space that allows for infinite intimacy.

Meditation:

If more than one is participating, perhaps one person could guide the meditation.

Allow the image in…that you exist in a world of Light. The Presence of Light is everywhere present. Feel the gratitude for that. Feel it. Feel it even more deeply.

Become aware of your breath. Allow awareness of deep and rhythmic breathing. Take a deep and slow inhalation of that Light, and on your exhale, allow that Light that is your very Self to grow as a glowing and radiant sun. Allow yourself to behold it radiating spherically through yourself, bathing each illumined cell. Behold it streaming forth as sacred liquid light, as a sea of Infinite Love pouring forth from within. Feel it. The key is to deeply open to feeling this Presence of Light. Feel the joy and even the rapture and ecstasy that you are. That you Already are! Each cell is an illumined cell.

Be aware of your Self as Light...emanating from the center of your Being. Feel that Light. Identify with that Light. It is your Self...the only Self. Merge with that Light. Be One with that ever present Light. Know this as your true Self. Open to this precious Presence of Light.

Be aware that you are bringing awareness to what Already IS! Light manifest as your very own Self flowing forth from in your heart, the holy of holies.

Be aware of the Light as a Holy Presence. Be receptive and open to this Presence. Be at One with IT. Relax and melt into this precious energy that is Everywhere Present. Allow time to disappear. Allow even your personal sense of human self to dissolve. Allow the timeless realm of Presence to be felt and known.

Be aware of the power that is this Presence. The only Power. And be aware of how your awareness of this Presence allows you to see it inwardly and feel it flow outwardly. Be aware as it does animate not only your life...but fully as all of life. The ONE Presence dancing as the Sacred Two, the yin and yang, in man and woman and in all of Nature and all of creation.

Be in the gratitude of this experience of Oneness, of Presence. Sincere and deep and wordless appreciation will increase the experience...for it activates the law of gratitude which is a law of increase and supply. It opens wide the doors...

And exaltation comes...

Partners in Purpose

The Sacred Two. Man and Woman. What thoughts and images and emotions come forth from humanity about this dynamic two!

From the history of rising and falling decadent civilizations right up to the present moment, the balance between man and woman has been the unequal, impotent, and even insane foundation of these civilizations. This very imbalance is the breaking of the inviolate and inexorable Universal Law of Balance.

No wonder…the falling of civilizations.
No wonder…the fear and pain and suffering.
No wonder…the wars…the conflicts.
No wonder…that true cultures of light
could not emerge with harmony.

The Sacred Two is OUR story. It does seem personal. It is impersonal. It is the Undivided ONE come as the Two…ever longing to reunite as the One.

This is the stage. The playground. THE Movie! And it does not have to be a pain-filled human drama created in seeming separation from the ONE.

So what did compel me to create this oracle art book about these Partners in Purpose… these Star-Stone Twos?

I was deeply inspired by Presence. The seed was planted early as I entered into a family of classic imbalance. Although my mother was a wild woman tap dancer, boogie woogie woman pianist, and one of the pioneering woman pilots taking to the skies with a sense of immense freedom, she was never able to keep the balance in the home. The societal "unspoken" stay in your place of submission was clearly there. The male domination was firmly in place. I saw the freedom and I saw the slavery.

My mother says I spent my first three years smiling and joyful. By age four I had a glimpse of "man and woman" in balance via my very childlike wonder. I was enchanted that it was possible. It forged my choices as the years and decades passed. And I saw the imbalance in homes around the globe. The mirroring into the governments, nations, and businesses was seen. Masculine mind domination was the master most everywhere. It was a global imbalance.

My awakening has been gradual with periods of vast glimpses. It has provided a way to integrate and understand with growing stability and understanding. After some immense awakening experiences in the 70's, I began to enter the realm of Original Archetypal Woman and Man during the 80's and 90's. I was not trying to "get there" in meditation. I was merely meditating on the One and that is one of the many doors that opened unto me. I was not asking for this awareness. It simply was what was unveiled. From unknowing to knowing. Many revelations of the illumined True Man and True Woman. Beauty Unspeakable! The ONE Light manifest in, around, and AS the seeming appearance of man and woman. Light AS.

During one revelation in the Realm of The Sacred Two, while I was at the base of Mt. Whitney, I beheld a divine procession on a high bluff of the sacred partners down through the ages, under the names of princes and princesses, kings and queens, priests and priestesses, and on. The ecstatic beauty and love was so illumined and immense that it was difficult to stay conscious. It awaits our knowing.

As more was revealed, I came to know that during this current time of grand awakening globally, we would see a new kind of man-woman, yin-yang relationship emerge. Partners in Purpose. That time of emerging balance between man and woman is Now.

Then the paintings, passages, poems, and sculptures began to come. Those have become this book, *The Sacred Two.* I now offer this book as a catalyst and inspiration and initiation for fine tuning one's awareness to the ONE as the Sacred Two. The Star-Stone Two. The Star-Stone Tribes. They do come. Inexorable balance does reign supreme in this spiritual universe that we do seem to know as this Earth, this world.

The book is an invitation to the Wedding…of the ONE manifest as the Star-Stone Two.

A Culture of Light emerges as pure Consciousness. And it emerges two by two. The Holy Presence, the ONE, appears as man and woman, as yin/yang expression, in all of Nature, the processes of Nature and in all the universe. Balance. It is the Law. It is inviolate. It is a priceless gift. This book mirrors that expression.

Passages of The Sacred Two

World Birth of Balance

I would like to share some of the story of how this book came to be.

I am four years old. I remember The Sacred Two. I do not remember in an academic, doctrinal or a sexual way. I do not remember in words. I remember with the wonder of a four year old. I remember with the innocence of a child. I have no doubt. I ask for the gift of a doll in a white gown. I am in the delight of my knowing...I do smile...

That doll would be my reminder for years to come. Those years included some stormy times and some doubtful years in the human story of man and woman...in the human story of miscreations and great imbalance.

History, of most all nations and civilizations, carries forward stories of the battle of the sexes and of the imbalance between man and woman. It carries forth the stories of the rise and fall of matriarchies and patriarchies in families, organizations, businesses, education, nations, and civilizations. The imbalance only breeds imbalance. Novels, mythological tales, movies, songs, poems, and true stories through time tell of their sorrow-filled stories repeated over and over. An endless cadence of the tragedy of imbalance.

We sit now at the edge of non-time. We sit between the form and formless, between the time and the timeless, between the ONE and the seeming Many. It is a play of grand paradox. And the mind cannot travel unto this non-place. It is ONE. There is no separation. And it is both wordless and nameless, though we give It many names.

This grand paradox is a state of consciousness. It is a holy Presence. It is the Undivided One that is the Divided Two. And It is ever seeking to reunite as the holy ONE... through endless giving and regiving.

It is the Nameless ONE.

Let us Remember.
Let us see It everywhere.

Let us see it in weather...in hot and cold...
Let us see it in processes in Nature...precipitate and evaporate...
centrifugal and centripetal and on...

Let us see it as rain does enter into the earth...

It is seen as a lizard stretches on a rock in the early morning sun...
It is seen in the polarities of all of Nature...
It is seen everywhere...
It is even heard when the sound of owl fills the space of dawn...

We can find rapture in the realization of all of life as an electrically sexed universe.

We can find joy in the awareness of this sacred dance of the undivided one, dancing as the sacred two in all of Nature everywhere...

Let us enjoy the dance...

I continue now with my seemingly personal story. My doubt-filled years...they did pass. I began to have experiences of deep rapture in the Silence of my soul. I began having spontaneous awareness in other realms. These realms are living and moving and feel more real than the apparent physical reality, so filled with global battles is it. These realms are revelations of life lived in wholeness...of life lived in balance. Through inner vision I was witness to ecstatic Realms of Archetypal HE and SHE. In this witnessing of the ineffable, I experienced unprecedented joy. It had no reason. Just purity of joy.

During a period of years, I was aware of this state of consciousness, this holy presence in many different ways. Early one dawn as I lay in my bed, union did visit in yet another way. Sky did enter my crown and Earth did enter my feet. And yet again, the coming together, the merging, the union of polarities felt. In the marriage of earth and sky in my body, they came together in my heart and waves...endless waves...of orgasmic unconditional and universal love did fill all the cells of my body. My consciousness was pure love. I was the Holy Wedding. Yin and Yang within my being as a great celebration. Love was known as Impersonal. It just IS.

In another experience, a lucid dream, vast numbers of serpents entered my crown and my feet. They also merged in my heart. There was an instant when they first entered the heart when I understood Infinite love. I awoke from the dream with waves and waves of the unconditional love flooding through my being.

Through only a glimpse, one's life changes totally. One comes into an awareness of holy Presence...that is love. It is. That is all. It is whole. It is complete. It is perfect. Past and future...they do fall away. And one's physical world begins to shift. What has been life becomes Life. What has been seeming as one's personal story is experienced as an Impersonal Story. The personal and Impersonal. Again the paradox.

My life in separation from Oneness had now opened to a grander glimpse of Life. The

One Life. I was open even more to holy presence, that awareness might grace my life, as in the living of the epiphanies I was witnessing on the inner planes.

I had been painting since the sixties. I was now expressing in order to give form to the Formless and give visibility to the Invisible. I wanted only to continue living the awareness that had opened to me and was upon me. I would begin by sharing that Consciousness in painting and sculpture. I was experiencing Universal Soul. I desired to infuse that feeling into my art. At times I was overwhelmed by the inspiration to share what I was experiencing in those uninterrupted moments of bliss and satori. Returning home from Sedona, Arizona in 1987, I stopped at Mt. Whitney to enjoy the mountain, the rocks, and to go into the Silence. I drove past the rocks. They were as silent, giant sentinels lining the road and I felt I was being invited again into another expanded state of Consciousness. It was yet another deeper invitation to the wedding. I closed my eyes while still in my car and my inner vision opened. I sat in awe before a giant, open and cavernous mouth, with the tongue fully out.

Only later did I realize that it was like unto the primal mouth at the center of the Aztec calendar. I had a certain knowing that I was to enter into the darkness of that formidable orifice. I did. At first it seemed I had entered the blackest void. The following scene did appear. From the right, high up on a beautiful bluff of a mountainside, a processional began. There was a walkway, leading to I know not where. On it was man and woman. Archetypal Man and Archetypal Woman. Archetypal HE and SHE...of all Creation. They began to walk on this processional path in pairs. Two by two. In pairs did they come. The priests and priestesses of old. The kings and queens. Princes and princesses. Shamans and shamanesses. Regal, royal, and beauty-filled. Noble beyond measure. Here walked Beauty beyond the mortal mind. It is always here. Waiting. Waiting for us to know...to be...

It is everywhere present. I had trouble keeping conscious, so great was this Beauty walking by. Here walked Beauty SHE and HE from mythology, from history's lore, from all times past. Yet they were here. They never went anywhere. And we are the seeming them.

I felt I was witness to a calling forth, a heralding of the divine origins. And it was unveiled two by two. For many years, I meditated on this. I saw that we are moving into the creation of a civilization that will not rise and then fall from the great imbalance of male and female. I saw that we are moving into a creation, borne of balance of yin and yang. The Sacred Partners lead the way in the formation of that culture. Two by two. Two by two do they bring forth the children in Love. Two by two they bring forth children of balance. And two by two do they bring forth the Ideas/Visions of a new cosmology. The Sacred Two herald the way.

The Sacred Twos! They are the fulfillment of the fairy tales and the myths. They are the sacred balance. They are the law of love. They are the yin and yang of all creation. They are the dance of Life. And we are that.

The seeming battle of the sexes is no more than a playing out of the belief of imbalance of man and woman. It is no more than the mistranslation of the Dance of the One as Archetypal HE and SHE. Each of us is the possibility of that dance of the one as the sacred two. Even the butterflies, with their short lives, do find their life partners, through their antennaes. They attract their partner through the frequency of light.

And it became very clear to me that as we become aware of Presence that we shall live *and they lived happily after…and the story begins.* The real fairy tales will be lived. And they are being lived by many.

Enter...the Fairy Tales

On October 22, 1998, as I was out walking in the morning this insight came to me.

The world is as a true fairy tale. And, as in many fairy tales, there has been a curse or a spell.

The world, humanity, just like the fairy tales, is under a spell. The spell is the human sense of separation. The spell is the cloak of forgetfulness that comes when we humans left the kingdom, the consciousness of the heaven world, the unity, the union, God.

From that moment we have lived in separation, which is fear that causes untold pain and suffering. It is the concepts and beliefs of good and evil...everyone disagreeing with each other.

How do we break this spell? Did all the great illumined teachers...such as Krishna, Buddha, Laotse, and Jesus break the spell in their own lives?

Why is it we have not found the way to break the spell...and to enter the kingdom...as in the fairy tales...and live happily ever after?

Desire to enter the fairy tale...the kingdom. This desire is the first step toward entering... the fairy tale. It is the first step in this pilgrimage to the holy of holies that is without place or time. It is within...

Tell the Women...
Your Wedding Day is Now

child...
tell the women they need not battle to get their man nor to keep their man.
That battle...dear children...is the battle formed of unconsciousness.
It is the battle of desperation.
A battle of no home and no tomorrows.
It is a battle formed in the human mind in response to emotions of great imbalance.

Tell the women that the battle will end only when they find their own balance.
That Balance is found within.
It is the energy of the ever sought kingdom within.

Tell the women they will never find that balance in an outer man.
They must seek marriage.
They must seek union.
And that wedding awaits within...
It is the wedding that ends all the battles.
Seek the beloved within.
Enter into this great union.

Tell the women that then...he can come...

HE...it is...who will feel her...
HE...it is...who will know her heart...
HE...it is...who will long for her...
HE...it is...who will find his way...

O woman...worry not...fear not...battle not...
Be in your union...
Prepare yourself inwardly for this outer marriage.
Know you not that the outer marriage
is only a reflection of the inner marriage.
If you have not the inner marriage
how can other than a sham show up in your world...

Go now…prepare…
Prepare ye…
Prepare your temple…
Prepare your garments…
Prepare your inner space…
Prepare the wedding grounds…
Prepare in joy and anticipation…
Prepare for Him…the Beloved…
The Bridegroom…He comes…

And tell the women…they need not try to find him…
They need not search for him…
nor chase or pursue him…
They need not study astrology…

They need only to find the Presence of the One within…
Does it sound too simple?
Begin to walk this path of the Inner One…
Desire this union…
Let all your passion infuse this union…
and behold…

It is not possible to do the outer search
while doing the inner union.

Choose.

And should the choice be the Wedding to the One…
begin to watch, observe, behold…
Your wedding will begin to show up everywhere.

You shall wed the trees that blow in the wind…
You shall wed the sweetest mountain flower…
You shall wed the streams and waters that flow
through your body and all creation…

Behold…at last the wedding…
Your wedding day is now…

Wed the stones, the lambs, even the beetles that be…
Wed the very air you breathe…
and the very wind…

The wedding has begun.
Your wedding has begun.

Tell the women their wedding has begun
when they join in holy union with the inner beloved.
Others, they will join the celebration…
They will behold an event of they know not what…

And they will come…dancing…singing…
They will join this mystery…
of they know not what…
They will join…

Yea…it is a mighty paradox…
In this great inner marriage…
lies your outer marriage…
I say…yea…it is so…

Begin your walk to this marriage altar…
…with reverence
…and passion
…and knowing

And be aware upon this outer walk…
You need tell nobody…
Everybody will show up…
We are One…

Life's Dance of Polarities

The collective consciousness has not been ready for The Sacred Twos. The collective has been experiencing much pain and suffering of the imbalance of mismating for human purpose and desire for ages and eons. Each one will come to see that one cannot "process" with the "wrong mate-partner" to make it the True Love, the Partner in Purpose, divine purpose. Each will come to see that he or she must come into union with the Inner Beloved. That union will attract the outer beloved. As within, so without. That is the law. That is how it works.

Many of the animals that mate for life are examples for humanity. But humanity fails to see the Life, it is, that brings together such true partners, not fashion, politics, tradition, games, lust, loneliness, war coups, religion, and all the other miscreated social reasons to come together.

Life itself brings True Love together. True courting is a divine play of energy, a dance. It is the dance of Life itself. Observe the courting of the birds and animals who mate for life. They perform ceremonies and dances with these energies of polarity. If one is attuned to the subtle energies, one may feel and appreciate and enjoy this courtship. It is pure joy. It is the energy of the oneness come into precious form as the Sacred Two. Courting is the first play, the first dance of the Eternal in the relationship of Balance.

The SHE and HE dance the Dance of Balance. It is an exquisite movement of the Infinite.

On the human level, there are often so many personal opinions, desires, controls happening that the Infinite has no room to play. A courtship has no space. It has been suffocated by human desires and miscreations. Sex often becomes the place where partners try to get something from the relationship. And this lustful exchange comes in place of the beautiful and delicate exchange of the divine dance of unconditional love.

Let us come into the dance of polarities, where exists the play of opposites, yet no opposition. Where exists balance. The balance that Already is!

Together...let us dance...

The Wedding Chamber: Holy Alchemy Already IS

Quantum physics, chaos theory, scientific formula, ancient alchemy,
and Presence…holy Presence

Holy Alchemy may be present in one's life at any age, any education, any profession, race, or religion, and even any place.

Holy Alchemy happens in Consciousness.

People speak of retrieving the soul. There is nothing to retrieve. Wholeness Is! Find where that is so! Consciousness of the Invisible, Undivided One allows Life, Vision, gifts, talents, God qualities to stream through you, as you…without a human and finite sense of separation…All blocks, all obstacles, all problems are in the human mind as false beliefs and concepts. The mind must be transparent to the Presence… How is that done?

First it is good to understand that to indulge any longer in this false sense of separation in one's mind will only be the bringer of untold pain, suffering, and misery and misfortune upon one. Separation does breed fear, and these pains are the offspring of fear. When we get even a glimpse of this…we will begin to look for ways to break down and dissolve the habit of indulging and entertaining this human sense of separation that seems so real. We will look for "our own way" of breaking and dissolving the human spell of separation.

We may bring our mind into the original state by dwelling on the Infinite, the Undivided Invisible, the Unmanifest, the Oneness, the simplicity of the Presence. We shall then learn to dwell and live in this grand substance of creation. In this substance is the Elixir, the Essence, the Wine of God's creating.

It is the fulfillment.
Touch…gently touch that substance…and it will begin to flow…

It will flow in, through and around and as you and It will fulfill.
And it will draw nigh unto you that which is yours.

That which is already yours.
This substance is the holy presence.

Dwell there and behold the alchemy that you feel and then observe...as your life begins to shift and change.

This is the Master Alchemy, for it works with no trying, no struggling, no controlling or manipulating. Not even managing. It is that which we often term magical or mystical or synchronous. And it is simply the mystery unfolding and unveiling Itself. It only needs to be tapped and allowed. When we open to It, It knows what to do. It needs no instructions and commands and long lists. It already Is.

We can be our own living Revelation of what Already Is! Surprise!
It already Is.
When we open to It, we allow It and we may just Be.
Being is Presence in action, in form.
The paradox manifest.
And it is good.

So the question arises! How do I open? How do I allow? Find a way to enter deep into the Silence and deep into the Stillness that Is. There are no vibrations or frequencies here. You have entered the void, the zero.

Here, the holy alchemy happens. Here you enter into the wedding chamber of which the outer wedding is but a mirroring. This sacred space of the inner marriage is the cauldron of the alchemy from on high.

Here there is no yin and yang.
Here there is no lover and beloved.
Here there is no separation.
Here dwells union...
Here dwells the truth of I, the truth of I AM.

From here, Mystical as Practical is borne. It is a grand birth. It is the World Birth of Balance, of yin and yang, of the masculine and feminine in all of Nature. And It is good. There is nothing but good, for we live in a balanced universe.

Only is it that the human mind, with its never-ending false concepts of human good and bad, continues to block the flow in individual and collective lives. We will learn to see through the conceptual blinders as we make of our mind a transparency through which this presence of light may shine brightly. Then we shall quit looking even for portals, doors, windows, and openings.

We shall receive more and more glimpses of the radiance that Is. Already Is!
We shall comprehend why God is called Omnipresent.
We shall see and feel Presence everywhere.
We shall behold this Presence in everything, in the kingdoms and the elements…
in all that we imagined unholy and unclean.
We shall behold…beyond the seeming, beyond the outer appearance,
beyond the effects world we live in, beyond the finite sense of good and evil.

In this Silence where Presence does dwell, rapture and exaltation await. They do not offer altered states, trances, or momentary light. They offer the truth of what Is. Already Is!

Rapture is the alchemical marriage. It is what humanity tries to do outwardly with alcohol, drugs, medicine. Even in sex, does humanity search for the alchemical union.

We call it by many names. But it is nameless and it is wordless.

Together…let us open to the alchemical union.
Together…let us render this mystical marriage.
Together…let us Behold the wonder of this quantum physics in action.
Together…let us enjoy the collective rapture of this global revelation.

The epiphany…is here!
The collective epiphany…awaits…

Realm Beyond Problems

Following is shared a simple reminder of what we may do when we feel a sense of separation or a problem around our partner.

When you appear to have a problem, what can you do?
You may go to the realm where there are no problems.

A place where there are no problems?
It is not a place…it is a state of consciousness…
an awareness of Presence…

There is only a vast Isness that may be felt and experienced. It may animate us with even no question or problem, with simple awareness of its Presence. And if, anyway, we ask a question and we go into the Consciousness of Presence, we shall find that we translate what we then view as an answer or a solution.

It is splendid alchemy.
It is a clear awareness of Consciousness unfolding.
It is the magic acted out in the most simple ordinary acts of our daily lives.
It is precious.
It is the chop wood, carry water.
It is the foundation from which smiles shall beam from faces of the world.

We are the heaven world, while we act as if we are trapped in hell, when it is, that we are only trapped in the false concepts of the human mind.

Let us together…leave the seeming realm of problems…
Let us experience the grand alchemy in every situation…

The Wedding Sanctuary

If man and woman would stop the battle, the world would stop the battle...
Would man and woman stop the battle if only they knew how?
Or do they have too many human interests at stake?
And if they would stop the battle, how is that done?

Within us, as a humanity, is the heart and mind...
the yin and yang of our being...
They must be in wedded union...
How can that happen?

Where is this marriage found...
that may bring heart (feeling) and mind (thinking) together?

There is, my friends, a sanctuary where the wedding happens...
It is deep within...
It is placeless, yet we give it place...
It can be found...everywhere and nowhere...
It is a paradox indeed.
And it is always calling.

There is always an invitation...
There is always an invitation to the wedding...

The Inner Wedding

Child…you wonder why I would speak of The Sacred Twos to you. You know the focus needs to be placed on Creator, so why all this attention on True Mates?

Child…it is this way. Humanity suffers greatly in the area of human relationships. But it suffers most in the area of man-woman relationships. The devastation of consciousness in that area so entangles one's energies that those concerned cannot find the desire for inner union. That is the last thing on their minds. They will tell you, "I have problems. My problems are outer. I must handle my problems."

They do not yet have the awareness that those problems, especially in man-woman relationships, are happening because they have not been told the vital importance of the Inner Wedding. So it is…that the need for this information is great.

When the energies of the planet are not held in bondage in the entangled man-woman relationships, a new lightness and freedom will be felt everywhere.

This bondage of energy is witnessed in movies, TV programs, fiction books, nonfiction books, some traditions and religions, and some cultures. No need to write out the details. Open your eyes and look about you. It is everywhere. Humanity is fascinated with the pathology of the battle of man and woman. It is the revered plot of man and woman.

Even it is…that one will feel that individually or culturally…if he or she is in control… that all is well. All is not well. One is out of balance and unsatisfied. And the other one in control is not happy.

This area of man-woman relationship has been an ongoing plague…a great global disease…throughout time. It has been a living lie.

Man and woman must ponder this subject well.
They must choose to be guided from within.
They must both find wholeness.

For those who find each other, in wholeness, unprecedented new man-woman unions will form.

Those unions will be the subject of movies, books, conversations. The Sacred Two will be sought after worldwide.

Fascination for the pathology of unconscious partners will disappear into the great sea of knowing. A few here or there may struggle to keep the battle alive. Its death is immanent.

The Sacred Two will walk forward to reveal a new life...for everyone...

Truth Lived

What does it mean to have a friendship or a relationship based on Truth? Many relatings are based on a mutual agreement (which is often not spoken) that the full truth not be spoken. One person might not be ready to face truth in certain parts of their life. However, if you are ready for truth in all aspects of your life, then that changes the relationship. You can no longer support the lie.

One must then face the fact that the person may not want to be with you or around you anymore if you want only truth. So one must be ready to let go of certain friendships if that is what is called for.

Be ready to move into the next level of relating with a like-minded one.

We do not have to be stuck in relationships of any nature that do not face truth. If we have seen a higher vision, we must be true to it and move on.

It is one thing to unconditionally love a person; it is entirely another to stay stuck in the lie with them. To stay stuck in the condition is like *looking back and turning to salt,* if you have seen the higher vision, the promised land, the garden, the fairy tales. The other person may not have opened to the higher vision. If you offer truth and they do not respond, you must let them go…or pay the price.

Our responsibility is only to our truth of our highest ideals, visions, and awareness. Our freedom is in this truth.

Truth being lived is the basis of the new Sacred Two relationships.

Let Us Celebrate

This wedding embraces all traditions and all cultures
that have ever been, that are, and will ever be...
This wedding embraces true love between man and woman everywhere...
This wedding embraces true love between the masculine and feminine,
the yin and yang in all of Nature, in all the mated opposites,
in all the kingdoms, in the elements, and the conditions of weather...

We live...in an electrically sexed universe of the opposites...
divine complements ever moving toward one another...
in a powerful dance of the One...reuniting with Itself...

Friends...we are that union......we all are that union...

Together...let us celebrate that union of The Sacred Two...
given from creator...come together as the One...
yet paradoxically they are still the two...

In this...the Mystery stands unveiled...
that we may feel the Presence of the holy union of yin and yang...
of this single man and woman in the grander scheme of things...

Together...let us celebrate...

Mystic Marriage

We call the mystical…extraordinary…
We call it…altered and paranormal.

That which is natural, ordinary, normal…
is Life…is mystical…

We are the ones living in an altered state…
that which has been controlled, manipulated, tampered with…
altered until it is almost unrecognizable…
and we try to call it etiquette and polite and reasonable…
and correct social order…

The paradox is fully missed…
The magic…it is lost…
Innocence and wonder…are fully lost…

The paradox…
where the ordinary meets the extraordinary…
magic happens…
the mystical…it is…

An Invitation to the Wedding...

Words may cast a spell or invite you to the wedding...
May these words that follow invite you to the wedding.

Let us not mistake a powerful human mind for Presence. We shall become troubled souls traveling in worlds of mind unseen. We shall create magic and unending dreams and universes...missing always the wonder that brings joy streaming...out of who knows where...

A never ending stream of joy and music does beckon. From where does it beckon? From everywhere and nowhere. It is the mystery we seek in the mind of never-ending schools. Yet it exists in no school; it is not a curriculum, yet a school might point one there. But there is no place to point. It does seem I speak in riddles. There is no riddle, nor are there any questions, nor are there any answers. Yet if you ask a question, an answer, it is there.

Today...I am here...in joy again. Yet there is no here or there and there is no place. How then do I describe this joy I feel that appears from nowhere? A smile does cross my face, as even it did when I was yet a child. A smile borne from nowhere, about nothing external to me. Just sitting on a rock beside the river, wearing a smile. What else have I a need for? This smile does say it all and this smile does all the work. It hails and beckons and life does flow, just like the river that now fills my ears. This river is not outside of me...it is the river of my soul.

Long years have I dreamed of my wedding, thinking it to be with a dark-skinned, long-haired man sweeping me away to an island where coral reefs do make me sing...and dance does greet the day...

Now is different. I sit beside the river. A fly does land upon my leg, walking ever so soft. A gentle touch. It is what I have longed for only in him. He finds me now as fly. A sweetness do I feel...as fly does make its way on down my leg. Fly has heard me...or have I heard it? It has flown now to these words on my page, walking on them...sealing our union. Childlike, I do delight. Now there are three flies. We are having a wedding.

These winged ones come close, being ever so still that I might see transparent wings that glimmer in the sun, like streaming light. Now there are four. Childlike...I am enchanted with this "wedding at the rocks" with the river singing loud.

Five come. There is no food to pull them in. I have come here many times. The flies did find me not. Today is the day of my wedding. One could ask, "Why not deer or eagles or even the squirrels of the trees?" But flies? There are no buts. The flies are Life…or is Life…flies?

The Beloved of the wedding does come in many forms.

When the proposal does come…please do don your finest smile and sing a song out to the stars. And look about with joy to welcome all…who have come upon this day.

A bird sings out from high in the trees.
It heard the call and gathered close.
No invitations or stamps or rsvp.
Enchantment draws in close.
It sings aloud from the highest tree.
I see it and it matters not.
Its presence too is felt.

And am I a little girl dreaming again of the wedding, or now a woman who knows the wedding always was?

Beloved has flown to me today and whispered,
the wedding…ever Is…

The Wedding is Everywhere

I have spent many years with many men and many more with none. I seem to be the whore or the monk and nowhere in between. For a time, I was a midwest mrs. and even that came to a close. The dream of union never came; I thought it was with a man.

The union I sought is everywhere. In bright open day I see the rain does kiss the earth and enters deep within. I see the wind caress the tree and the tree does a holy dance. Even I can see the rare mountain flowers open their faces for touches from the sun, drinking nectar from the sky, lovers jubilant that the day's begun.

Lovers trysting everywhere should I care to see. Hiding not my eyes…I see the union everywhere. The wedding's everywhere. A smile does come upon my face…that I'm at the wedding now.

Upon my journey home this day, I watch the clouds embrace the mountain top. The mountain in its joy does disappear, returning later drunk with love, glistening and moist with new fallen snow.

I have witnessed this electrically sexed universe for many years. I have known the yin and yang that dances both silently and wildly through all of Nature. And today another veil does drop…and the wedding…it does appear.

The Holy Presence of Love

The Holy Presence of Love is before you,
behind you, above you, below you.
It is everywhere. It is abundant.
And it is yours.

It beckons from behind the scenes of man's imaginings.
It beckons.

It awaits.
It awaits your holy sight.
It awaits your holy hearing.

It changes all things in a twinkling.
All manner of thought turns to dust
and borne is the pounding of love that fills your heart.

And you do see that it fills all life.
For this Holy Presence of Love is Life...
and It is everywhere.

I come from nowhere
and I go nowhere...
and I am everywhere.

You seek me only on dark nights
between the sheets and between your legs,
yet I tell you...I am everywhere...

Begin to see me thus...
for I am everywhere...

You dream I lie hidden only in another's heart
when I am everywhere...
You dream that you need to find me
when I am everywhere...

There is no other…
I am everywhere…

You cry silently in the night
because you cannot find me…
yet I am everywhere…

I say…find me in the beating of your heart…
Feel my presence there…
Get very still…
that the clamor of the world falls into silence…
Let it die away…

And there I am…
From here…you feel no need to rush around…
to hurry here and there…

Litany fills your ears…
and you sleep and dream…
I call you now to wake…

I am in your breast, I say…
and I am everywhere…

True Power

Predawn, one morning, these two words do come to me…power…love.
Upon intently listening within, this thought does also come…
The people of Atlantis, we read, misused the power, misused the crystals.

Then comes the thought…if you have really gone deep enough within and touched the God within, the Power within, then the Power of God uses you. You do not use the Power. The Power of God is Love. It cannot be misused. Love cannot be misused. It is the Life force that uses you. You are only the instrument, a vessel through which this Power does live and move and create.

The misunderstanding of True Power is what causes the belief in the misuse of power, be it in ancient Atlantis or be it in the world as we know it today, including what we regard as male or female power.

Let us gather now in a new understanding. Let us perceive true Power, with a capital P, as the Life Force of that which we know as love. Love, dear ones, cannot be misused. It can only be "cast upon the waters" and it will return to you. Give and you shall be regiven. That is love. Allow that love and Life will bloom.

The understanding of true power is missed in its utter simplicity.

Power is covered by economics, statistics, predictions, graphs, and charts. It is covered with ancient endless stories of magic. All of those are the mortal mind trying to figure it out on the physical level. It can never be figured out from that level. Never.

For It, Power, is the outpouring of Spirit, Presence. And It cannot be measured. It is the Infinitude of Being and It will pour forth as you allow the love to flow forth.

Allow love to have a form.

When you seem to lie fallow in a moment of Earth time, you are both disconnecting from "human figurings" that bring naught and you are gathering in the awareness of this love. This Presence of Love is who you are. Let it flow.

Begin just where you are to let it flow. No matter how simple, how misunderstood, how unrecognized.

Let it flow.
It will find a resting place
and love will return to you.

Remember...love cannot be misused.
It only flows forth and uplifts all in its current.

Listen

On January 19, 2002 at three in the morning…these words do come.

I speak to those who listen.
I speak in a language they can hear.
I am simple and comprehensible.
I am ever present.

Never believe or even think that I am not here.
I am always here.
You must know how to hear me.
I am no secret; all the Ancients knew.

Even unto these times…I Am here…
for those who care to listen.
To those who listen shall come music unspeakable…
for all form does sing…
Music of the spheres shall fill these very lands…
Epiphany shall be on every tongue…
Sadness shall lapse from every heart…
Cries of delirium shall cease…

This music shall fill the air…
And upon their knees…people everywhere will fall…
souls melting into souls…
Unknowing ones trembling…

Gladness fills the air…
The new world emerges…
Prepare for gladness, friends…
Prepare for gladness…

I have chosen to include this passage, because it has been revealed to me that it is through The Sacred Two that the new world will emerge.

Spider Woman

I am woman. One day I flew into the sky.
There I saw Spider Woman.
SHE filled the sky.
SHE is vast.
I saw that SHE is "all women."
Everywoman makes up her legs.
I saw women from everywhere.
I saw women I know and ones I don't.
I saw all kinds of women.
I saw Everywoman.
Everywoman as one woman...Spider Woman...
who fills the sky.

I flew into what is called *mythological archetype.*
It is a living consciousness. And it awaits...
It awaits our seeing...

The women are dancing.
All are dancing the One Dance.
There is only One Dance to dance.

This is the land of great paradox, for each dance is different. Each dance is unique to the woman. And every dance merges easily with every other dance, like strands of Spider Woman's web...woven together into a moving, living, holographic pattern of the One Dance.

There is but One Dance...it fills the sky...

It was revealed as so simple...
So beauty filled. Enchanting.
Enchanting is woven by the enchantress.
And together they weave the world.
The woman weaves the world.

I am woman. Come.

Women everywhere must come into conscious unity, leaving behind the competition mind. Woman-SHE must realize the One Woman, Spider Woman.

Pre-tend You're in the Garden

Today, this moment, now…take time out.
Be a child.
Come play with me in the sandpile.
You may play anything here.
Come join me in the sandpile.

And let's pretend.
We pretended when we were children.
And we may pretend now.

Come with me as we explore the mystery of pretend.
Pre-tend. It is pre and tend when you break it down.
Children pre-tend their lives.
That is, they care for it, tend or take care of it…
in their inner world…before they grow up…
They are in their imagination (image in)
and they are in the physical world.
The world is as a garden…demonstrated…lived.
Children live no separation.

The real Garden/playground/sandpile is in our consciousness.
Children pre-tend there…so that it may come into their world.
There is no trash of conditioned mind in their inner Garden…
so they may pre-tend easily.

Let us now come into the sandpile…the Garden…
Make it like a smooth sand slate…
Still…without a ripple…
Allow yourself now to pre-tend…
that is…tend or care for…before…
Then allow that vision to "land or ground"
in the Garden…

Allow that which is Real…to flow forth
from the Substance of creation…into your life…outwardly.

The world…is within…

This passage is included to remind us of the Invisible Substance of creation and its appearance in the world of effects. Enter the world of…I Already have…

The Journey of No Return

The collective of humanity has not been ready to receive and to accept the science of The Sacred Twos.

The imbalanced relationship dramas of man and woman on this planet, in the garden, are diametrically opposed to the science of The Sacred Twos.

The Twos are a sacred fulfillment of the law. They are the promise kept. They are the rapture of the two as one.

They are the starting point for the emerging new culture. They are its foundation.

Those who know will quietly be birthing the Ideas/Ideals flowing ever forth from their Union with each other and with Divine Mind.

An alchemy is achieved by these Sacred Twos. A magic of incomprehensible joy and power of the Infinite is experienced by them. It cannot be feigned, hoped for, bought, or pretended. It either is there or it is not.

These partners in balance carry the combined qualities and attributes to bring humanity to new heights, unprecedented heights.

Joy and creativity fill the air around these Sacred Two. Their very presence is experienced. They are the fairy tales come true.

Unknowing ones run around trying to make these relationships happen. It will never happen that way, nor will it happen by endlessly processing and analyzing the miscreations, issues, and agonies.

It will happen when individuals first find the joy, ecstasy, love, and rapture of their own True Self. The relationship is then attracted as a fulfillment of the Universal Law of Balance, as the fulfillment of the ancient yin/yang circle.

Unknowing people chase the shadow of that fulfillment. They think they will find it in the other, in their partner. They will not. They will find it in themselves. And then the partner may come.

That inner rapture is then experienced outwardly, as well as inwardly. And joy does fill the air. Science in its ultimate form is at play. Science is the mental understanding of this sacred pairing. Science may explore this forever and have all the knowledge, yet never have the experience.

The experience is what humanity ever yearns, longs, and waits for. For it has a shadow of a remembering of the inner marriage that may unfold as the outer marriage. It is a sacred union. And it lies waiting at the center of our being.

It lies waiting for us to activate its existence in our lives...
It lies waiting for us to desire only the inner beloved...
It lies waiting for consummation...
It lies waiting for us...

And it is holy...
It is blessed...
And it comes...

Follow now the heart on the journey far within.
Listen to no man. The heart will know.
The heart will guide you on this journey of no return.
This is the journey that leads you from the shadow of unknowing
to the place of knowing.

This Place of Knowing is the kingdom of the heart
and it does beckon even now.
It calls our names...
It sings a sweet song...
It awaits your hearing...

As we enter this Place of Knowing found within the heart's kingdom of love, we shall recognize others who live also in this place of knowing. We shall recognize them through their eyes. Love shall shine from in their hearts. Light shall arc between our souls. Waves of love shall fill the air. And we shall know.

Words matter not. For in the deepest self...you have recognized the self, the one Self...in another. There is a silent pause for the communion of oneness. This place of knowing is a place of feeling. Information floods the waves in the feeling. Remembering the oneness is accelerated. Heightened awareness happens in this silence and the whole world sings.

This place of knowing is a dwelling place. A place to exist within the consciousness. It takes no time, nor does it cost. Rather there resides endless, Infinite love to be brought forth into ideas and forms and creations never dreamed.

O humanity, do find this place of knowing.
Ye shall see why it is called the journey of no return.
Who would ever dream of returning from this paradise of consciousness?

You say you would return for your loved ones. I say, they can't hear, nor can they see if you return. You must remain in the land of knowing. They will make their own journey when the burden of not knowing does begin to pain the soul. They shall wail until they cry out, praying deeply to know the ever-expanding vastness of the Kingdom of the Heart.

Make your journey now.

Portals into the Presence...

The Sacred Two oracle book serves to inspire, catalyze, reflect, and initiate the remembering and awareness of The Dance of the ONE as The Sacred Two.

As we each find the ONE within...we can recognize with holy sight, the One without. That is, The Sacred Two. When we discover that oneness, that balance within, it forever changes how we view the world, how we act in the world, and how we interact with all of Nature, that is our very own Self. There is but one Self.

And as we find the One within, we discover that I is not personal. We discover that I am Everywhere. I Am Everywhere present and I Am the only Presence here. The paradox heightens. And the awareness that comes is...the invitation to the wedding...that is ever present in all of life.

We come, sometimes but slowly, to the realization of Life as a celebration. Life as Living Ceremony. Life as a Dance of The Sacred Two.

In the realization of Life as a constant...invitation to the wedding...we see only the dance of love, only the dance of opposites as ONE in all of Nature. (Opposites yet not opposing.) There is always...only the wedding...

This oracle book is also...an invitation to the wedding. That union is Presence. May each image and each poem serve as a Portal into Presence...and upon entry may each piece serve to dissolve all human sense of separation...

Below find a list of titles of The Sacred Two, of man and woman and as the union. May they serve as openings...portals...into the realm of Holy Presence...May the names and words inspire and mirror expanded awareness...of who we are and why we are here...

Archetypal Woman

Priestess
Warrior Priestess
Shamaness
Divine Feminine
HER-story
Archetypal-SHE
Earth Mother
Queen
Princess
HER-Remembering
The Woman Dance
True Woman-SHE
Original Woman
The Silent Vessel
Seeress
Moon Goddess
The Mother
The Sea
Woman…the Dancer of Love's Dance
The Singer of Love's Song
Beholder of Beauty
She…it is…who Remembers…
Birther of New Forms
Star-Stone Essence-SHE
Changing Woman
Spider Woman
Sacred Passage of Beauty SHE

Archetypal Man

Priest
Shaman
Divine Masculine
HIS-story
Archetypal-HE
True Man-HE
Original Man
The Builder of Worlds-HE
Beholder of Truth-HE
HE…of the Sun
King
Prince
Seer
Warrior
Robed One
Knight of the Holy Sword
Sky Father
HIS-Remembering
HE…of Creation's Story
The Dance of HE
HE…of the Holy Thunderbolt
Sun God
Chief
Bringer of Odysseys
Epic-HE
Carrier of the Blade of Truth
HE…of the Sky

Archetypal Woman and Man

the alabaster marriage
the sky shall marry unto the earth
the royal twos…they build…
The Holy Wedding
The Sacred Two
Yin-Yang Circle…known of ancient times
The Star-Stone Two
The Holy Kiss
The Wedding Feast
Archetypal HE and SHE
Origin of the Twos
Galactic Shamanism
Return to the One
HE and SHE…of all Creation
Partners with Purpose
The True Story: the trustory
Dance of the ONE as The Sacred Two
Journey of the Stars unto the Stones
and they lived happily ever after…and the story begins…
Two by Two…shall they come…
Marriage of Day and Night…
Odysseys into Non-Time…
Sacred Union
Ye are the Sacred Dance
The Inner-Outer Union
Ceremony of the Twos
The Great Blending
The Great Wedding
Fairy Tales are True
World Birth of Balance
World Birth of the Undivided ONE
The Star Stone Ones
Marriage of Earth and Sky
HE and SHE…of all creation
Ancient Remembering of the ONE as the Two
Sacred Enactments of Ancient Remembering

Dusk does kiss the Dawn…
Earth and Sky Dance
Harps and Drums
The Garden already Is…
Land of Now
Life as Living Ceremony
Gift of Ceremony
The ONE Story
The ONE Vision
The ONE Dance
We are the living revelations…
Initiation of Fusion
Beauty HE and SHE…of all the fairy tales

Mystic Art & Poetry of SHE and HE

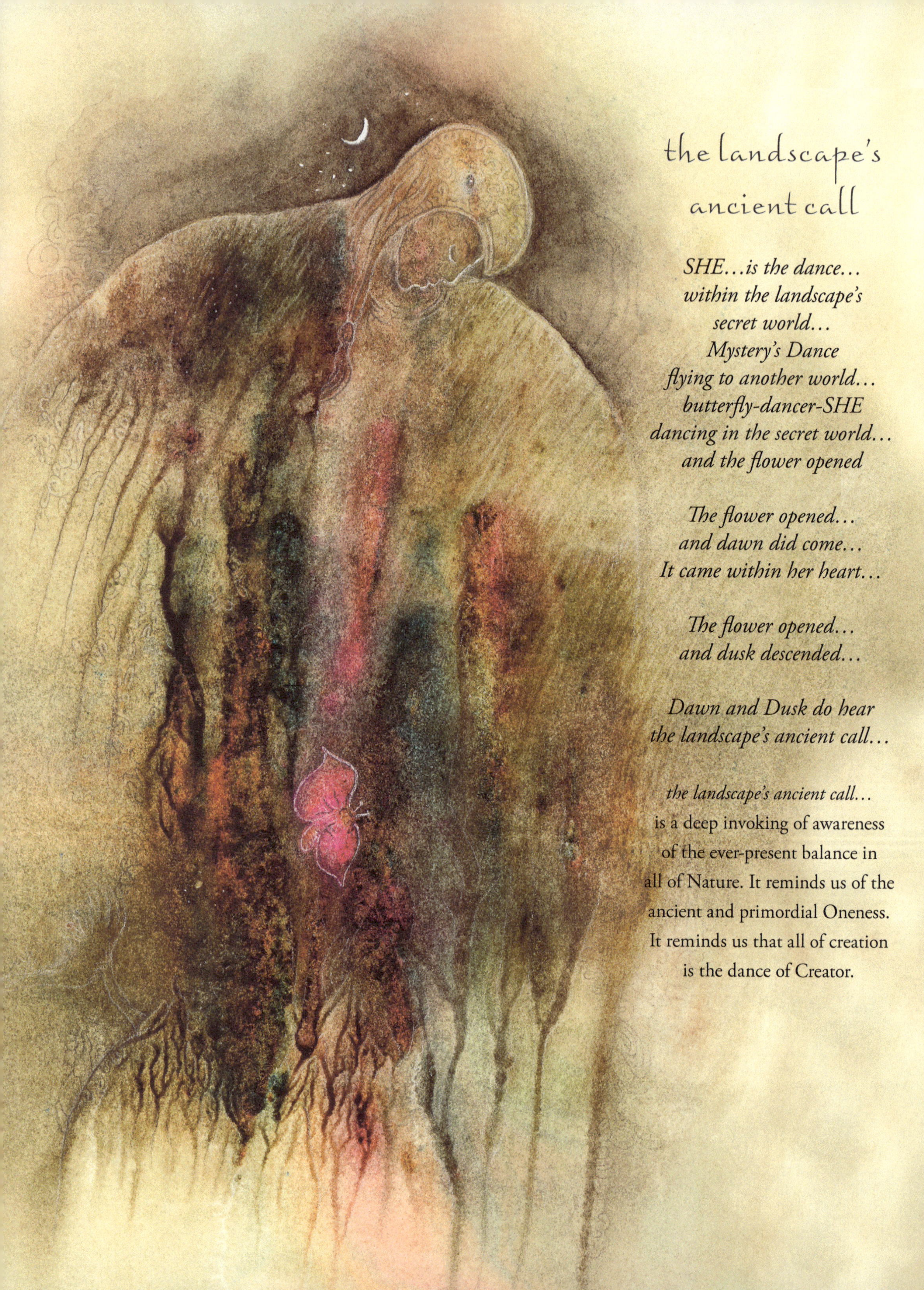

the landscape's ancient call

SHE…is the dance…
within the landscape's
secret world…
Mystery's Dance
flying to another world…
butterfly-dancer-SHE
dancing in the secret world…
and the flower opened

The flower opened…
and dawn did come…
It came within her heart…

The flower opened…
and dusk descended…

Dawn and Dusk do hear
the landscape's ancient call…

the landscape's ancient call… is a deep invoking of awareness of the ever-present balance in all of Nature. It reminds us of the ancient and primordial Oneness. It reminds us that all of creation is the dance of Creator.

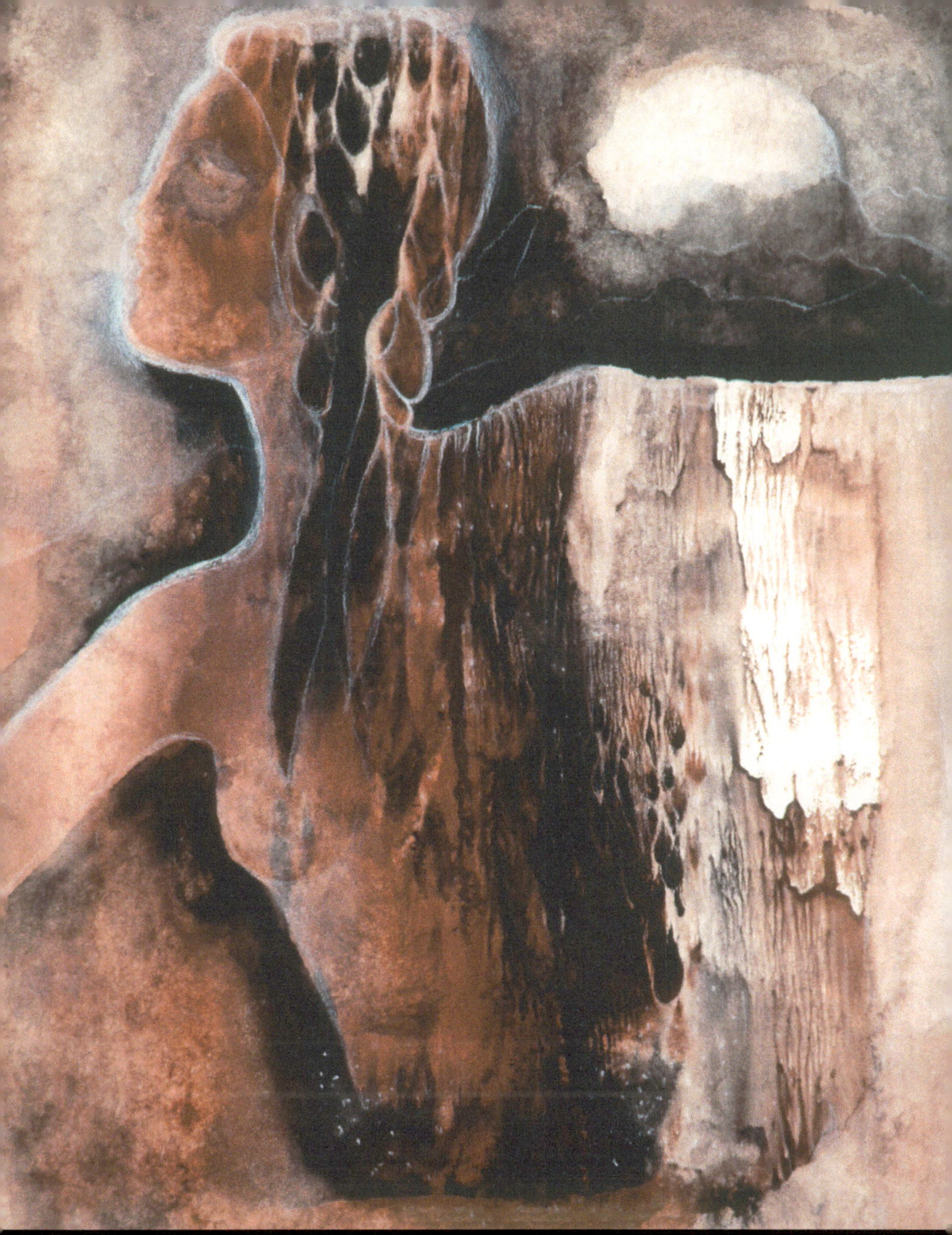

Starry Mantle of Spirit

wandering…
throughout eternity…
wearing…
starry mantle of spirit…
joy does fill my soul…

Starry Mantle of Spirit reminds us that we are ever cloaked in the Timeless Infinity that speaks only of the exaltation of Oneness

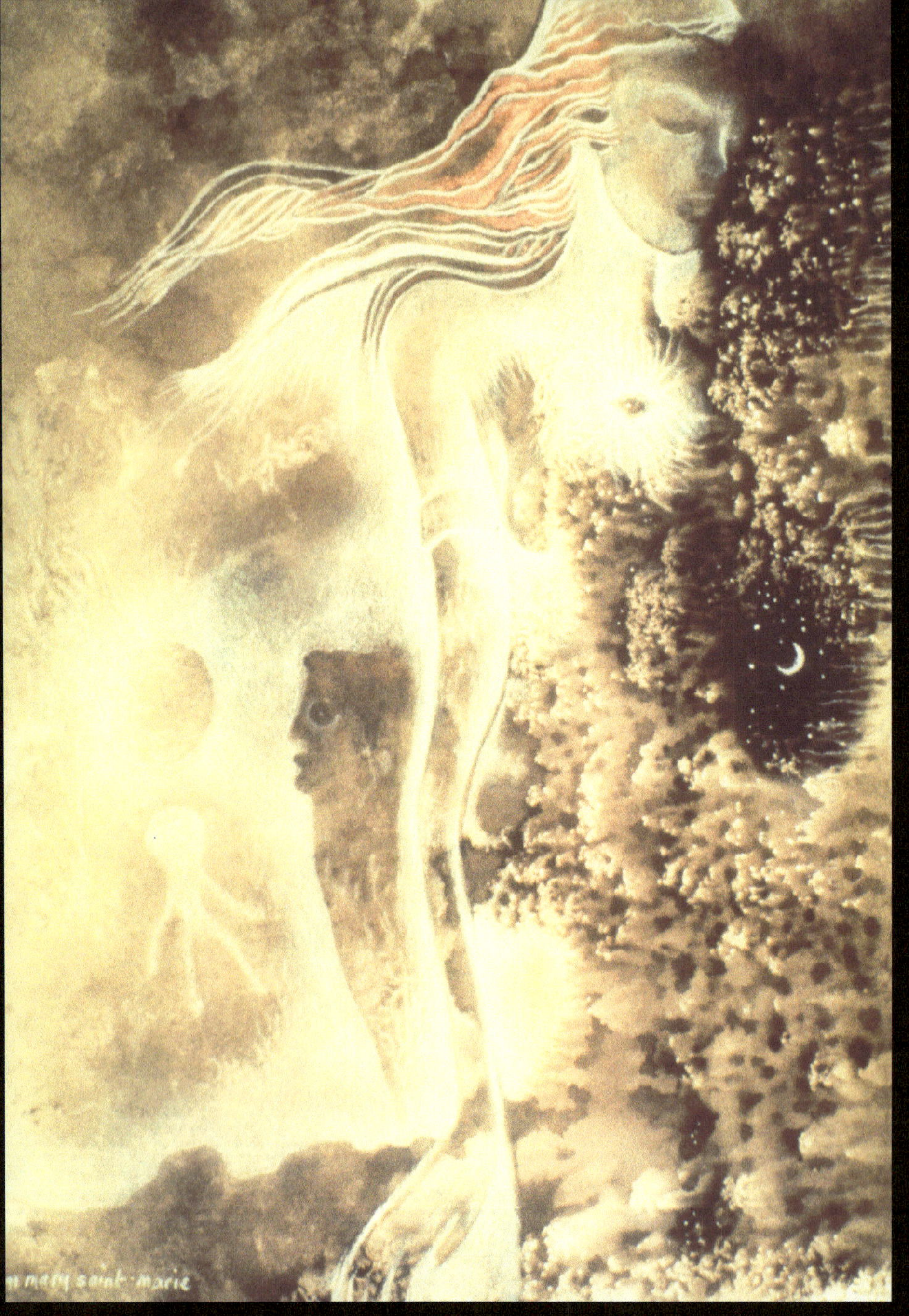

Star-Stone Essence-SHE

Star-Stone Essence-SHE…
O Maiden of the stars…
Come ye unto the stones…
…and Be at Home…
Far have ye traveled…
and there is yet a ways to go…

his painting calls to our remembering…our existence of the "as above, so below."

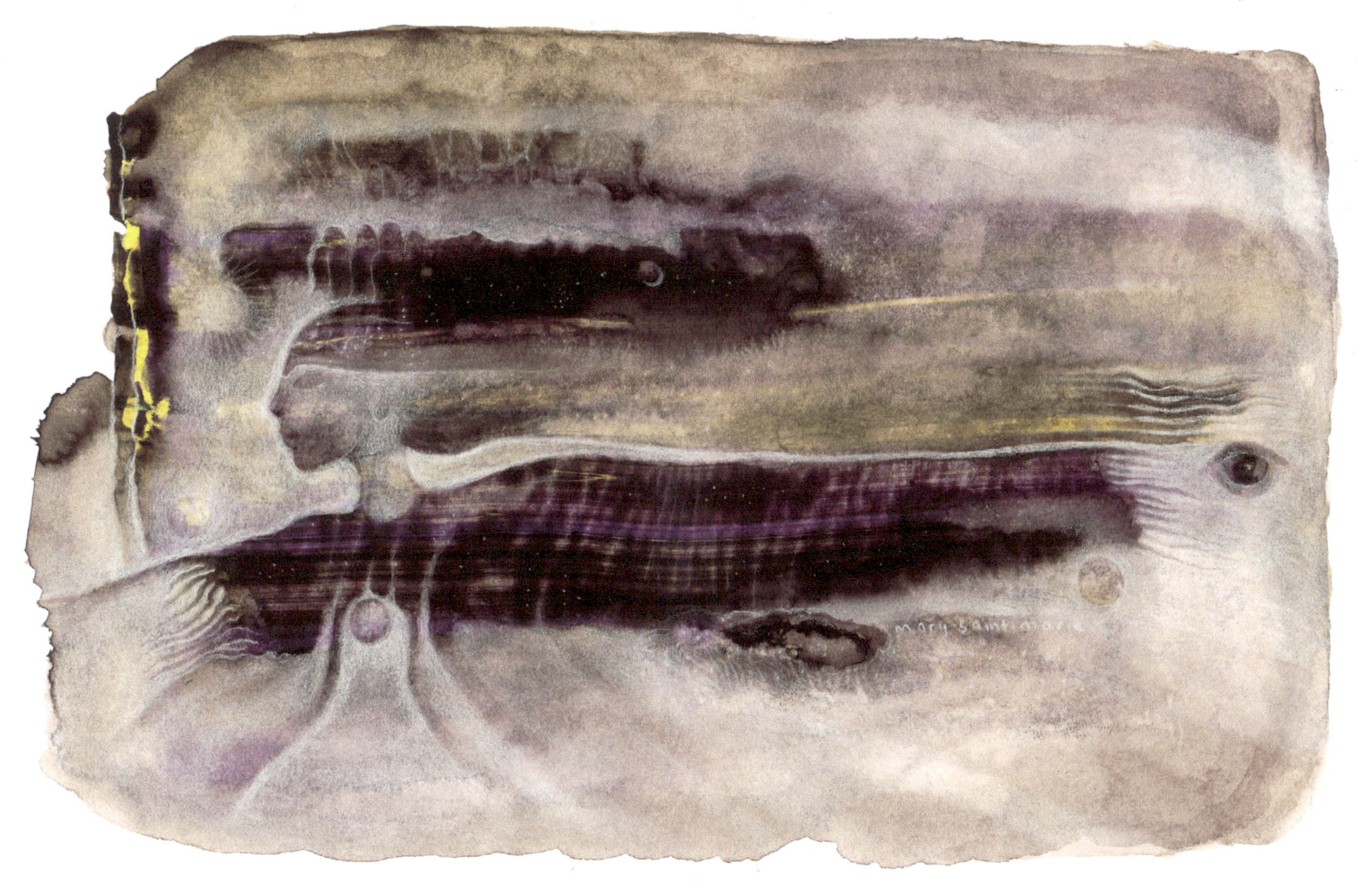

Spirit Majesty

for time does flee...
and leave us timeless in a world...
where we remember seeing...
seeing...really seeing...
seeing...we are those distant bluffs...
those stars...those moons...
symbols that surround our lives...

Spirit Majesty captures the timeless quality that we do glimpse beyond small mental talk.
It captures the unnamed quality that we do seek to fill our lives.
It speaks from the Silence...of the peace.

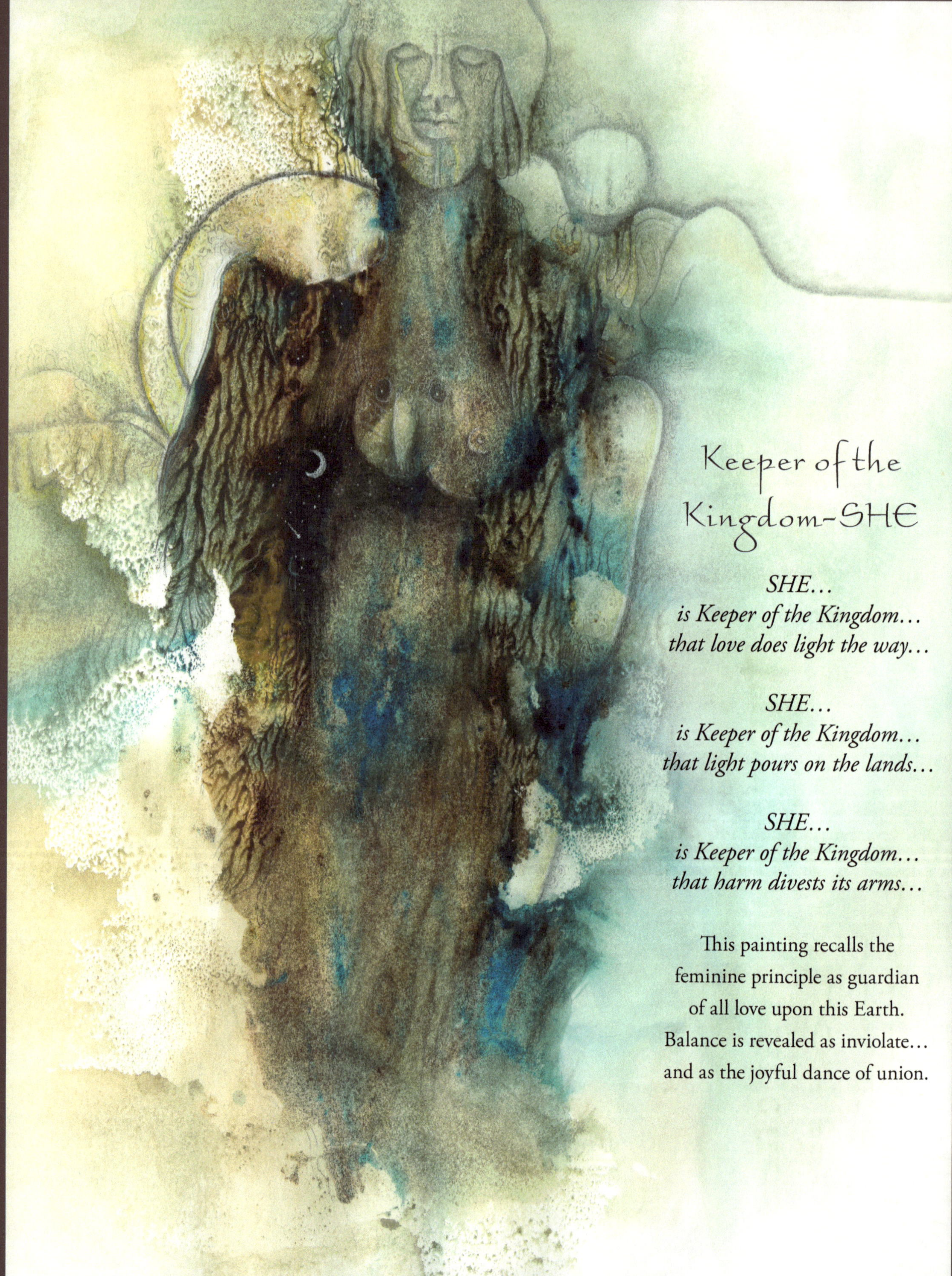

Keeper of the Kingdom-SHE

SHE…
is Keeper of the Kingdom…
that love does light the way…

SHE…
is Keeper of the Kingdom…
that light pours on the lands…

SHE…
is Keeper of the Kingdom…
that harm divests its arms…

This painting recalls the feminine principle as guardian of all love upon this Earth. Balance is revealed as inviolate… and as the joyful dance of union.

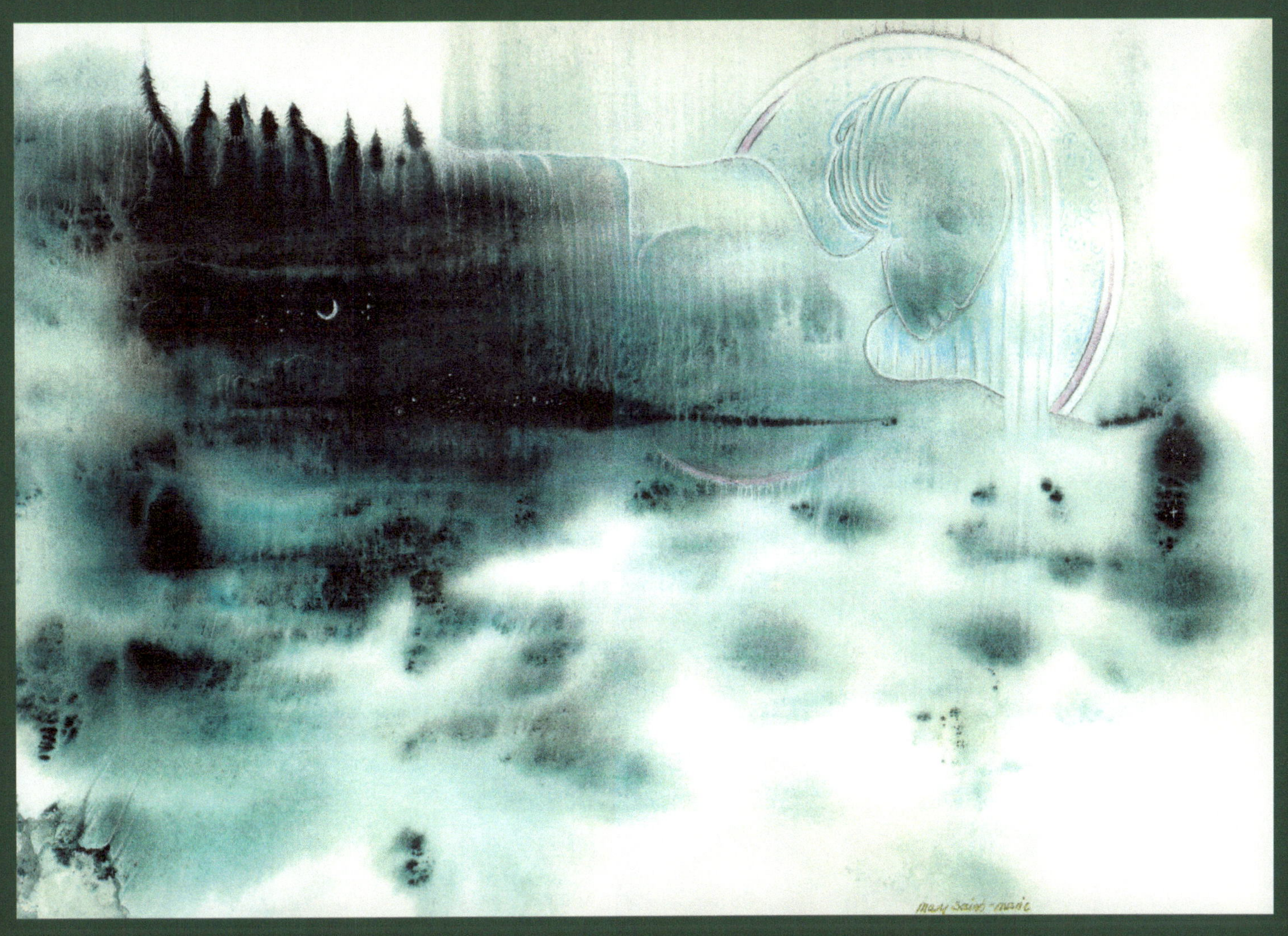

SHE…it is…who lies…
at creation's edge…

SHE…it is…who lies…
at creation's edge…

and knows…
that beauty guards the door…

Beauty stands at the edge of creation like a gargoyle…
a fierce protectress to all that is unlike HER. It is done.

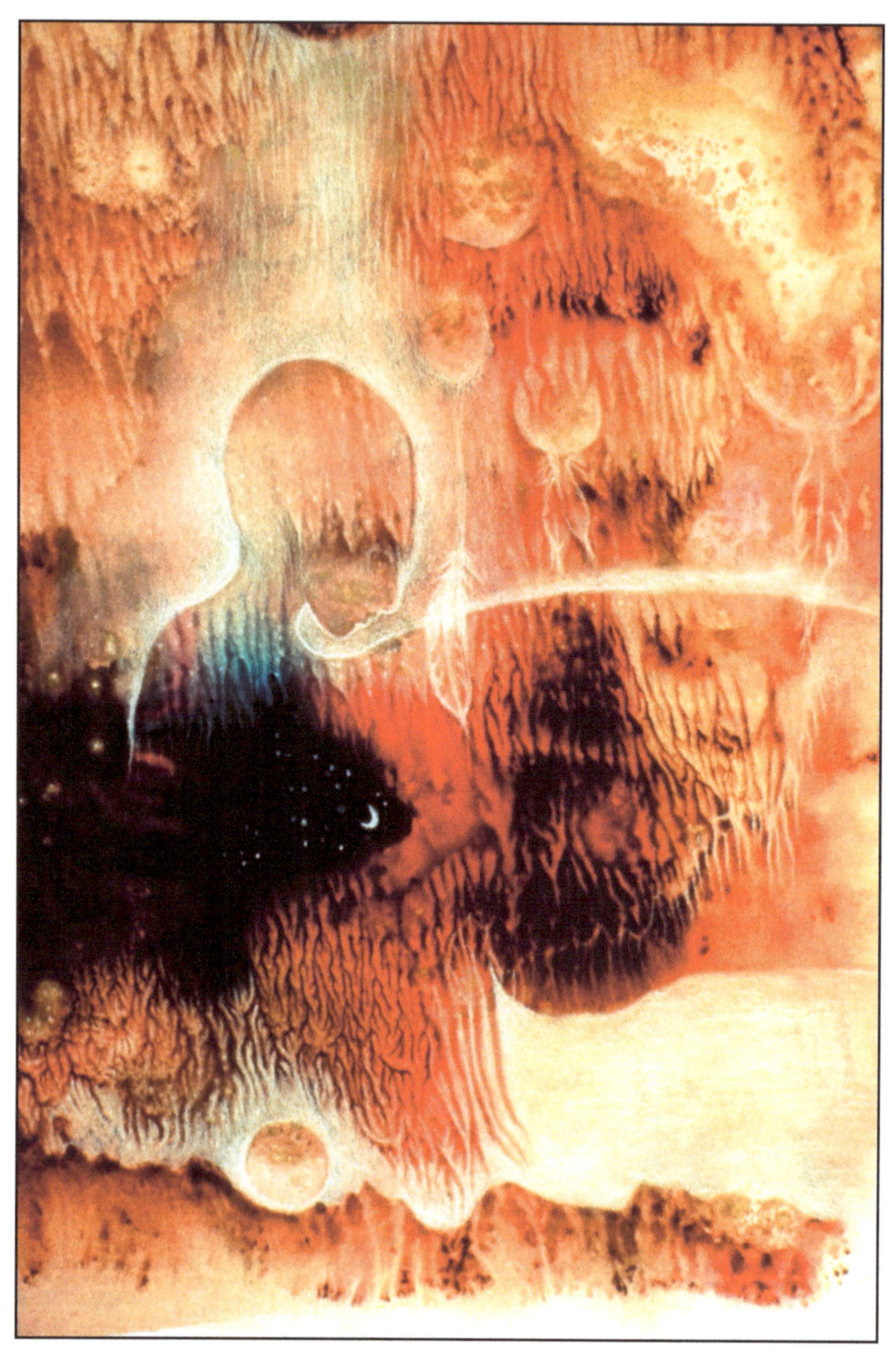

The Rainbow Dream of Beauty-SHE...

I do dwell ever in a place...
where inward...is outward...
a place where directions cease to be...
a place where the rainbow...
is a glow of white...

The land of separation ends in *The Rainbow Dream of Beauty-SHE.* The world of boundaries cease. And yet, forms, they do come and play.

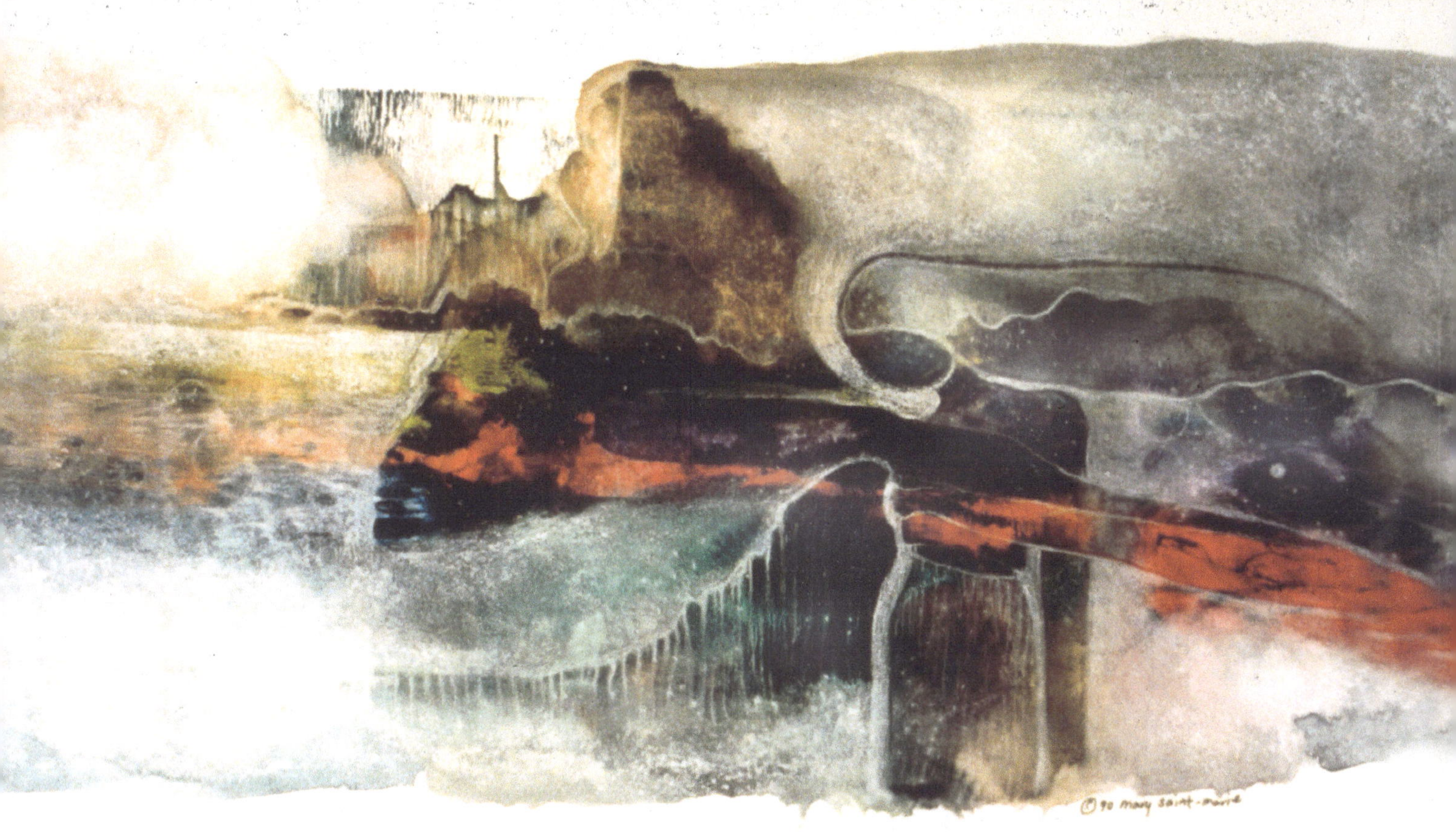

Beauty-SHE…of the Universe

Winged-SHE…filled with stars…
and many moons…
does touch the world…
with flaming scarf…
and beauty…it is there…

In this image, the world is seen as a realm of beauty. Let us see that Beauty is

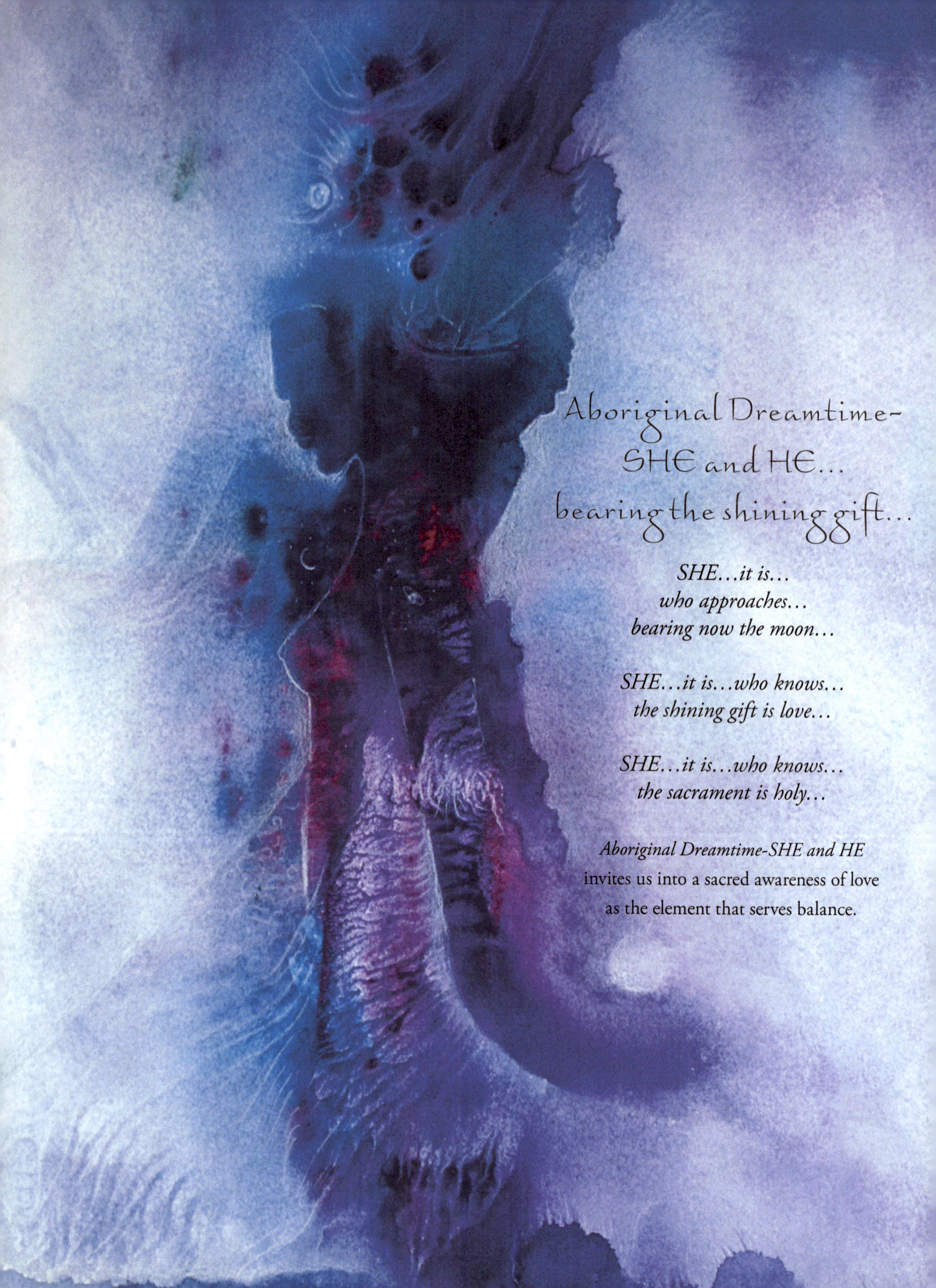

Aboriginal Dreamtime-
SHE and HE...
bearing the shining gift...

SHE...it is...
who approaches...
bearing now the moon...

SHE...it is...who knows...
the shining gift is love...

SHE...it is...who knows...
the sacrament is holy...

Aboriginal Dreamtime-SHE and HE invites us into a sacred awareness of love as the element that serves balance.

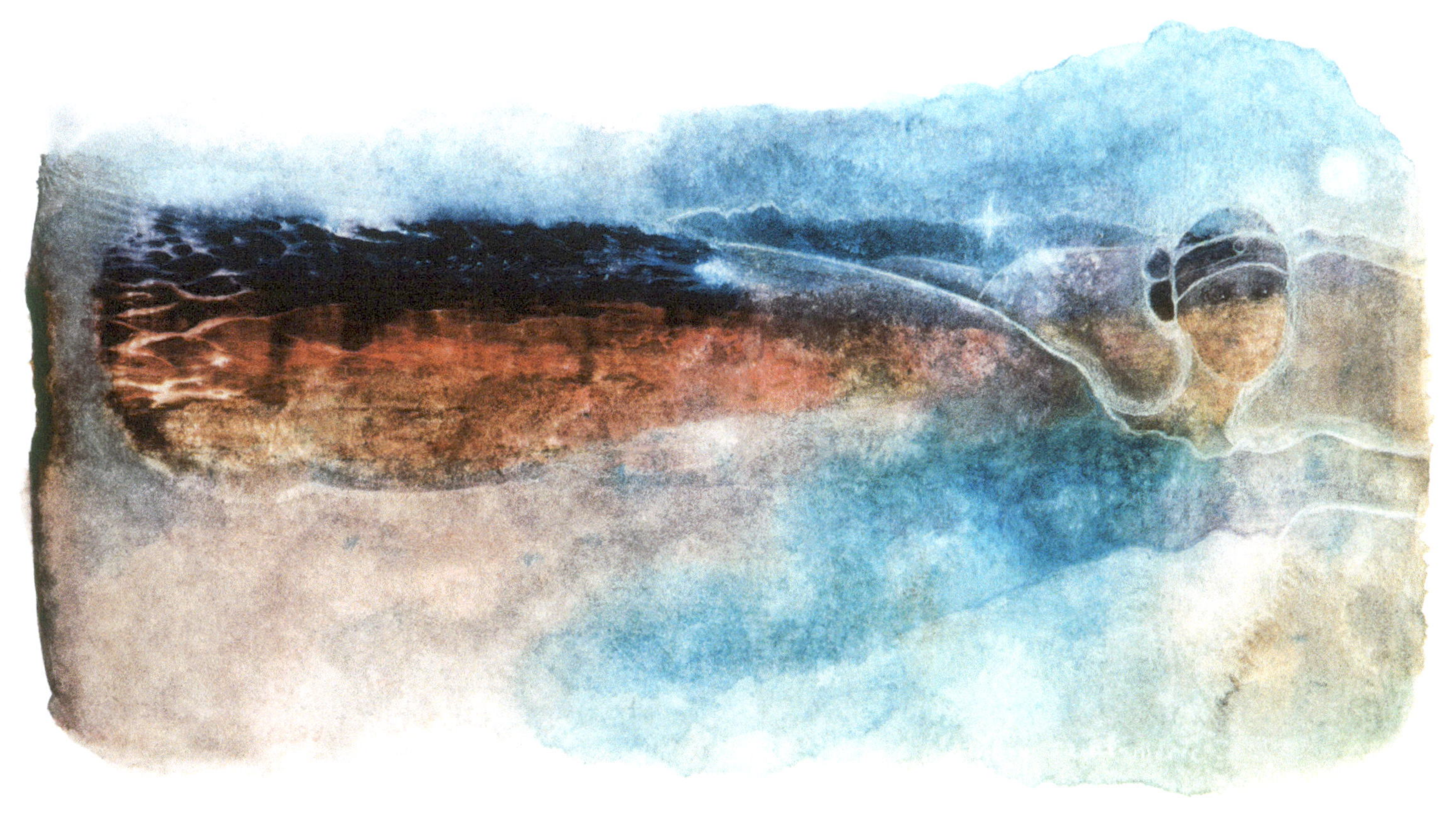

Rainbow-SHE...in flight

Rainbow-SHE...in flight...
o formed and formless is SHE...
a paradox in time...
landing but a moment...
telling of a shining...splendid self...

Rainbow-SHE in Flight represents the angelic presence of light all about us, in us, through us and as us.
Rainbow-SHE in Flight represents all the hues, all the possibilities, all the love...
Rainbow-SHE in Flight is connected to the starry realms of formless magic and to the mystery of Earth...the formed.

A story replete with the awareness of our lives in the visible and invisible realms is captured here in resplendent rainbow colors.

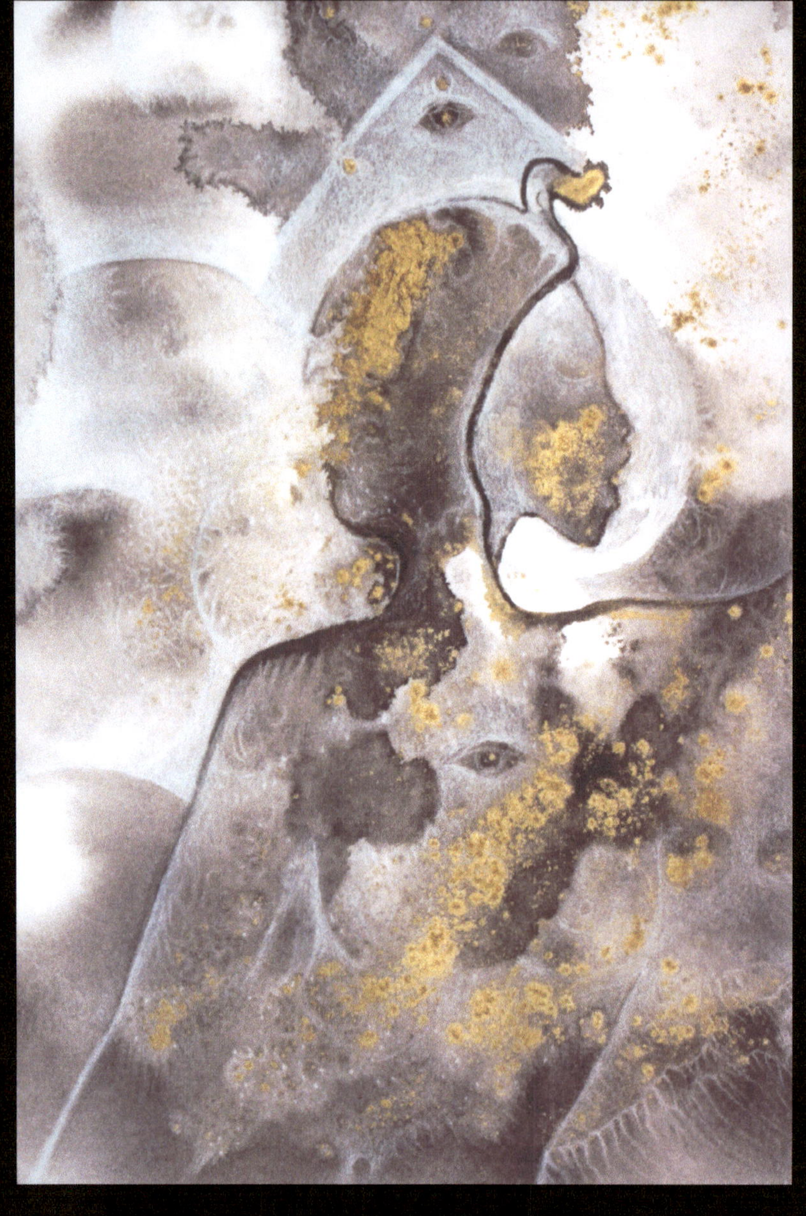

Golden-eyed Ancient Beauty-SHE

Golden-eyed Ancient Beauty-SHE…
sings the song of songs…
borne of the single eye…
dwelling ever in her mind…

Serpent wisdom rising…casting crystal light…

Towering temple…mirror to the Self…

Revealed here is the source of the song of songs…
desiring ever the rapture of release unto the world…

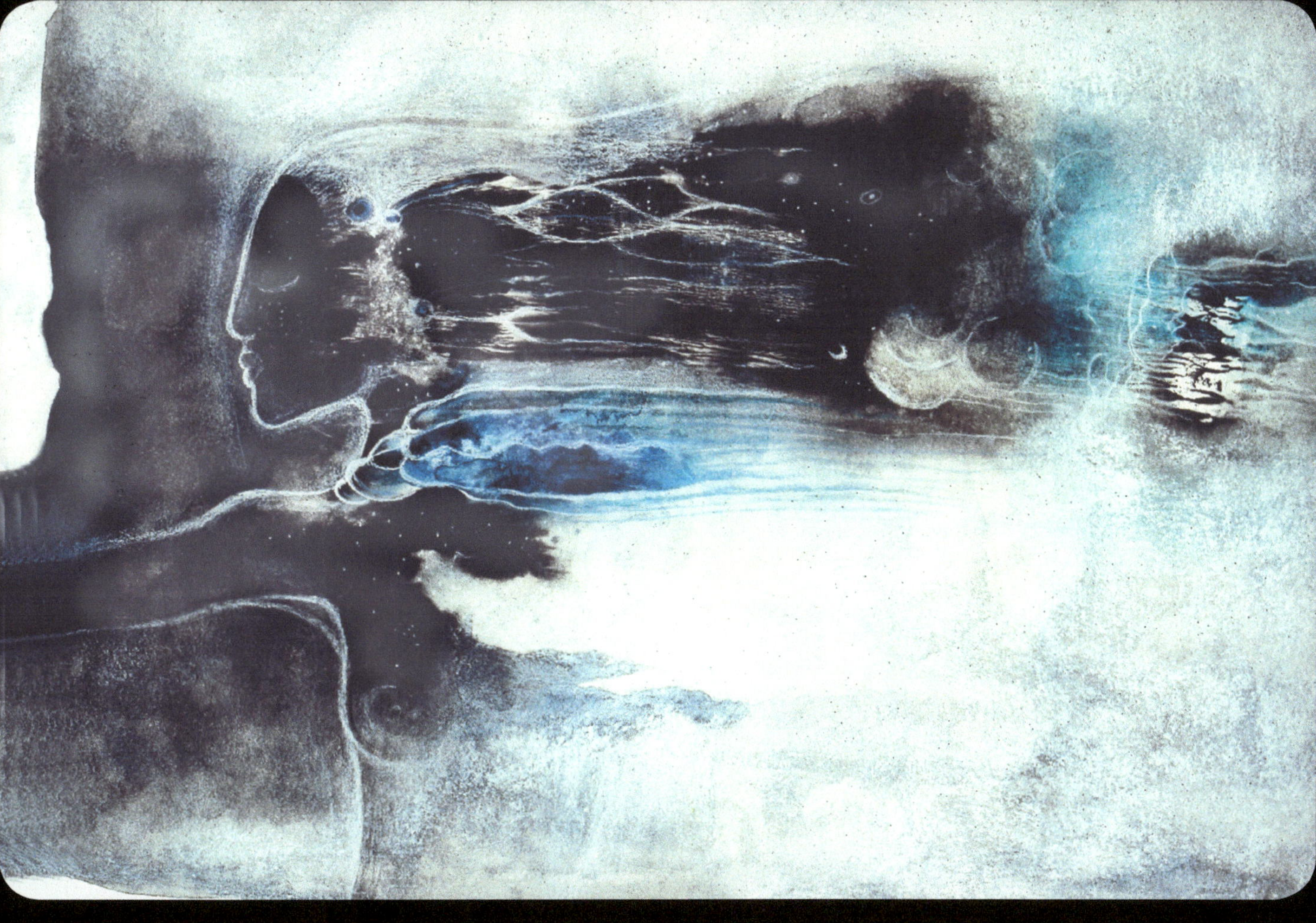

Journey-SHE...from the Stars unto the Stones

SHE...does make a journey...
from the stars...unto the stones...

SHE...does come a ways...
as a carrier of love...

Essence...sounding from untold realms...
here...to open wide the door...

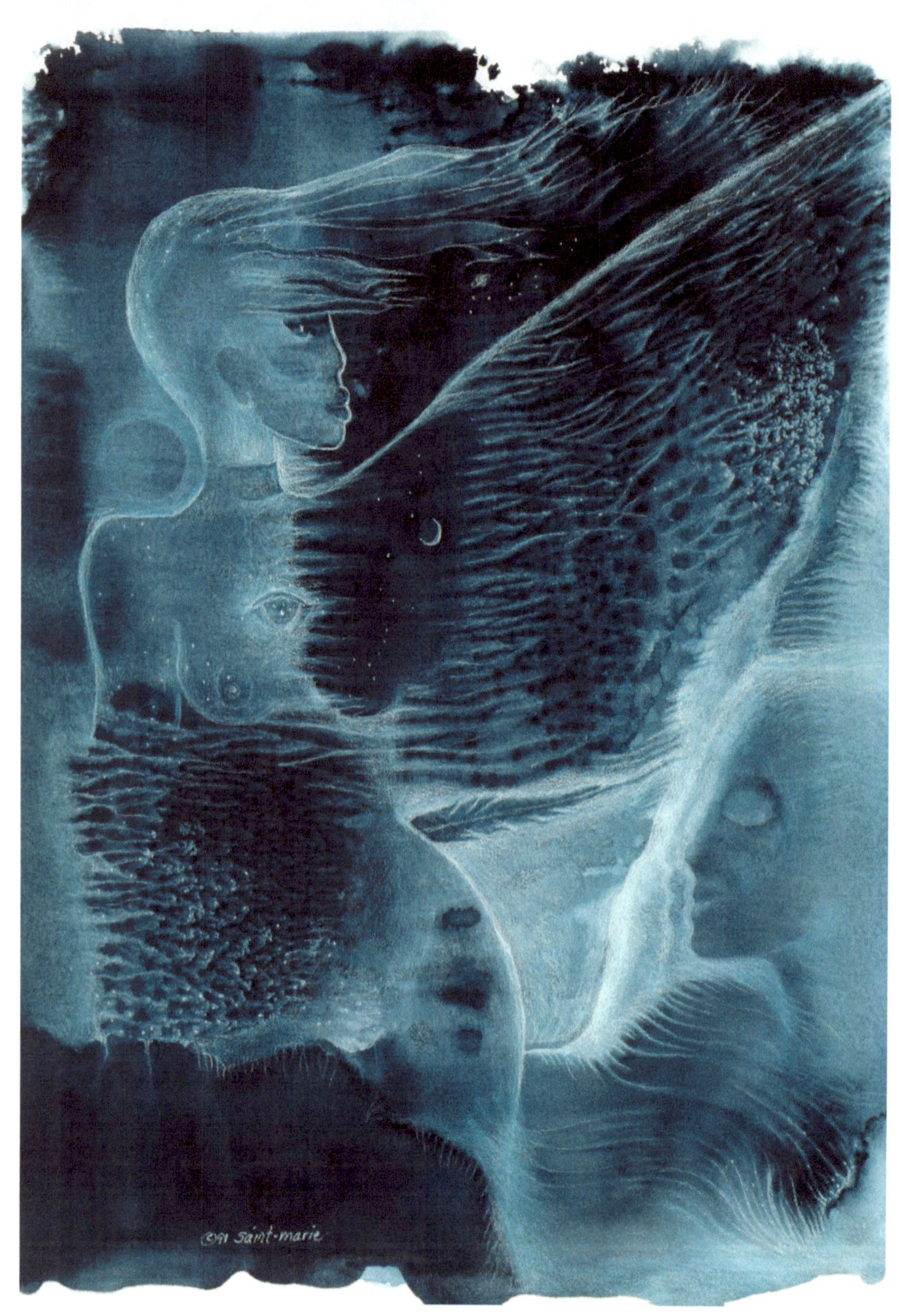

sky-dancer-SHE

sky-dancer-SHE...remembers the flight...
beyond the stars...
winged one...exploring forgotten realms...
returning with memories...
of a world that is now...

sky-dancer-SHE tells the story of a cosmic scout dancing forth to unveil that which IS! It IS!

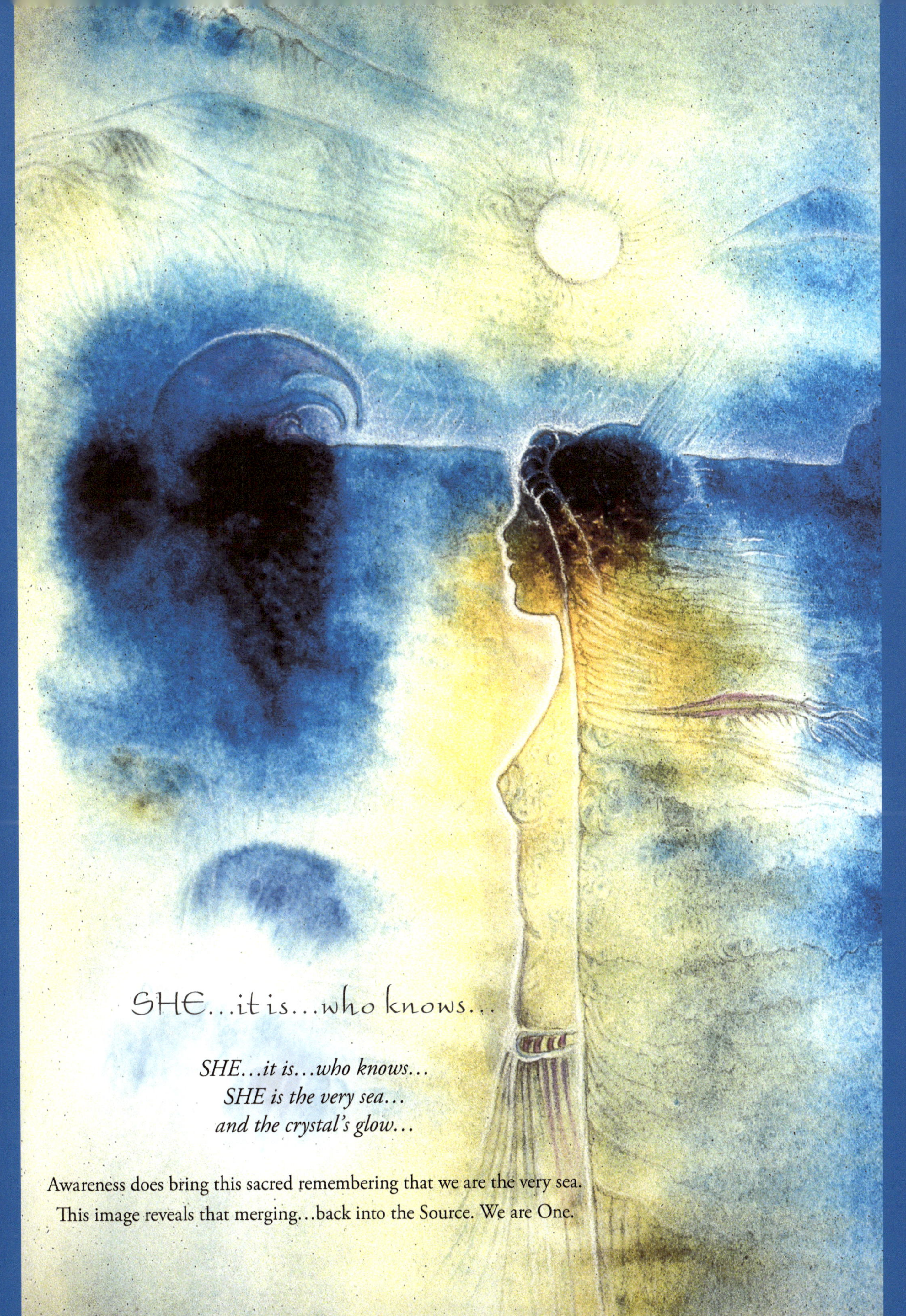

SHE…it is…who knows…

SHE…it is…who knows…
SHE is the very sea…
and the crystal's glow…

Awareness does bring this sacred remembering that we are the very sea. This image reveals that merging…back into the Source. We are One.

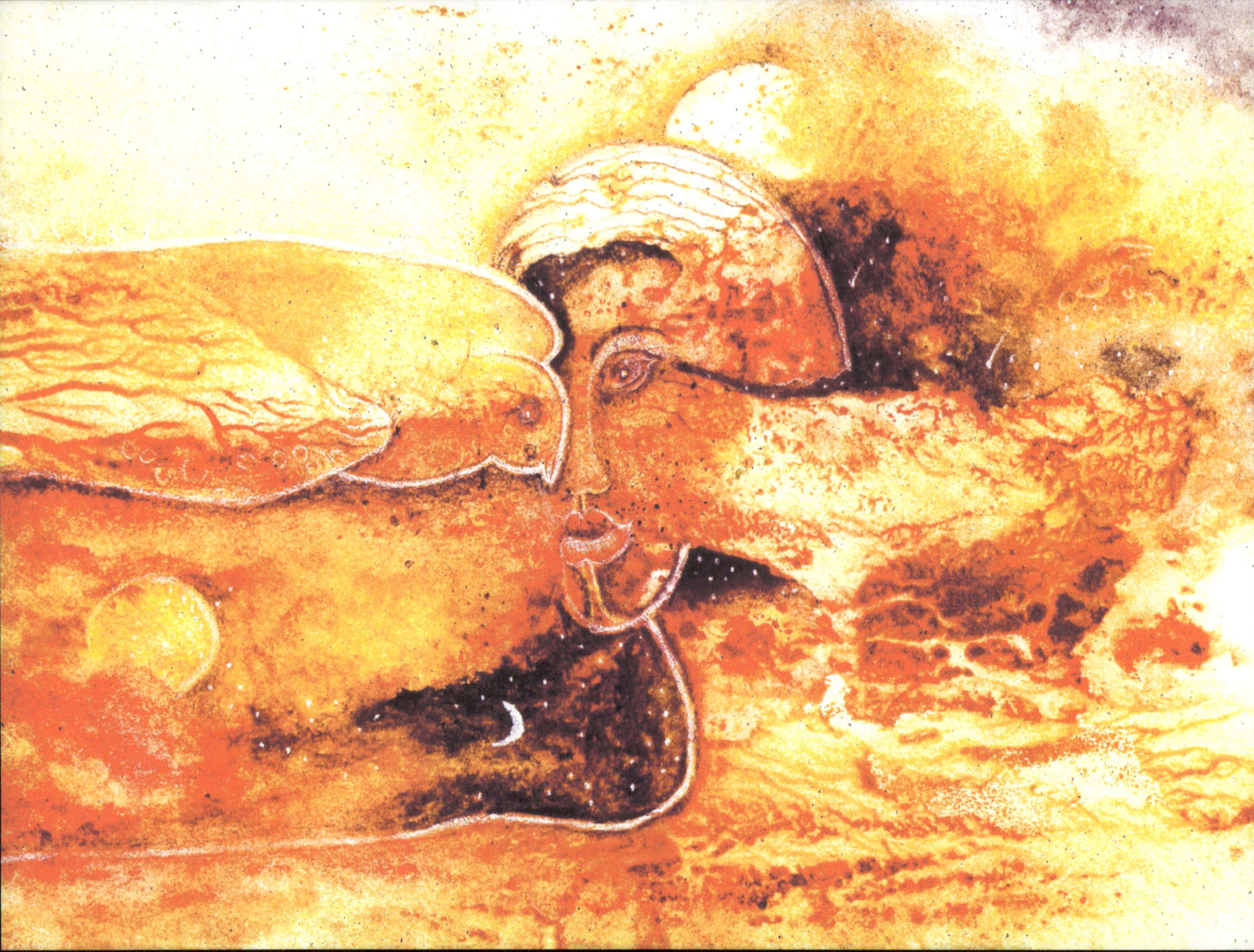

Ceremony with Creation

a flight to the mesa…
to remember where we are from…
a flight to the Earth…
to see the world of form…

Ceremony with Creation ignites our feelings of Oneness with all that is in our known universe…with portals into the unknown…

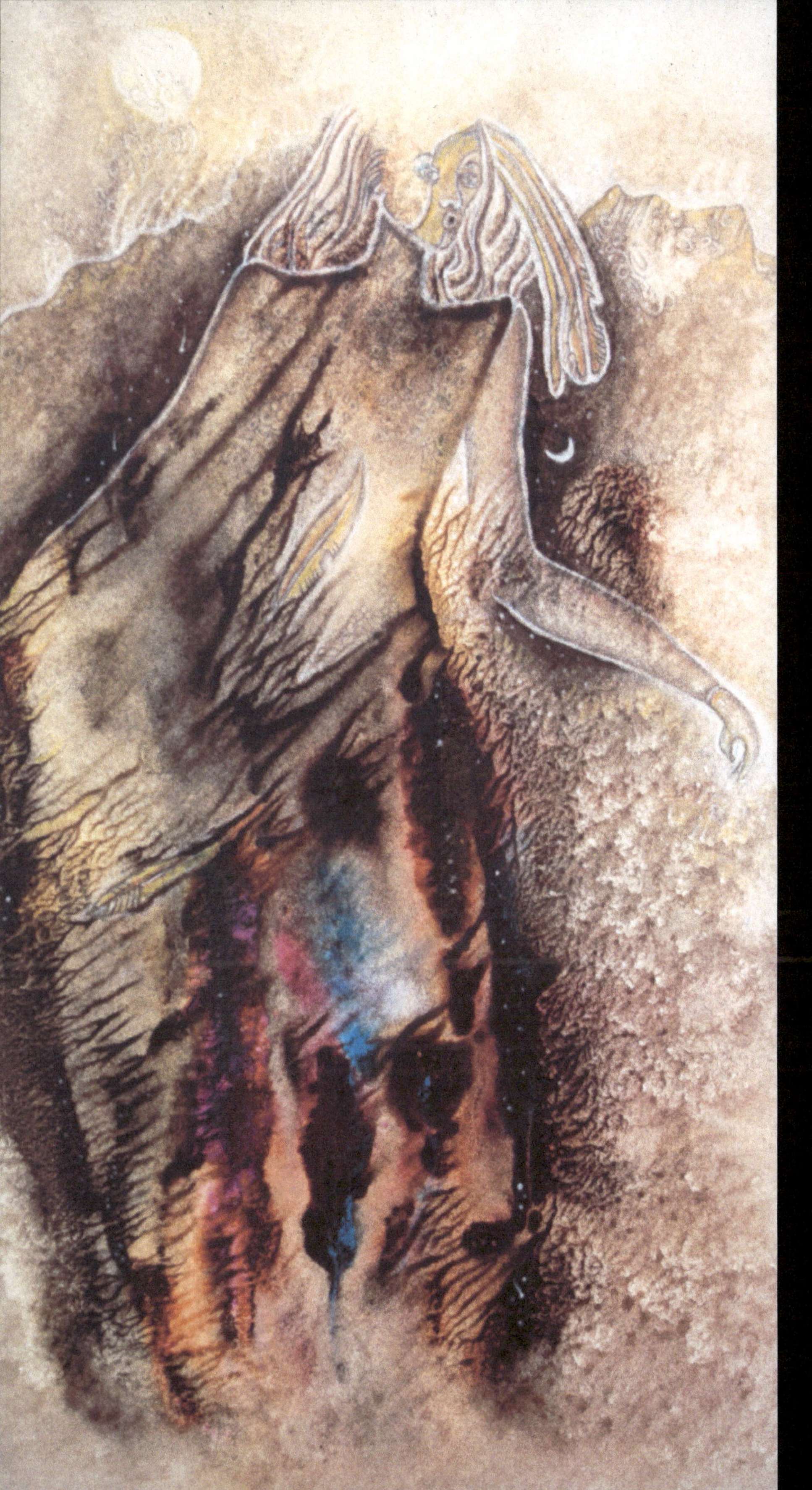

Song of Ix Chel: Rainbow Goddess of the Americas

I sing...
I sing of freedom...
of joy...
I sing of coming
and going...
I sing as the one
who does not die...
for I am...
married to the Light...

Ix Chel is portrayed in ceremony,
dancing and singing
as Mayan Rainbow Goddess.
SHE celebrates independence.
This is the time of the return
of spiritual consciousness.
SHE celebrates that return.

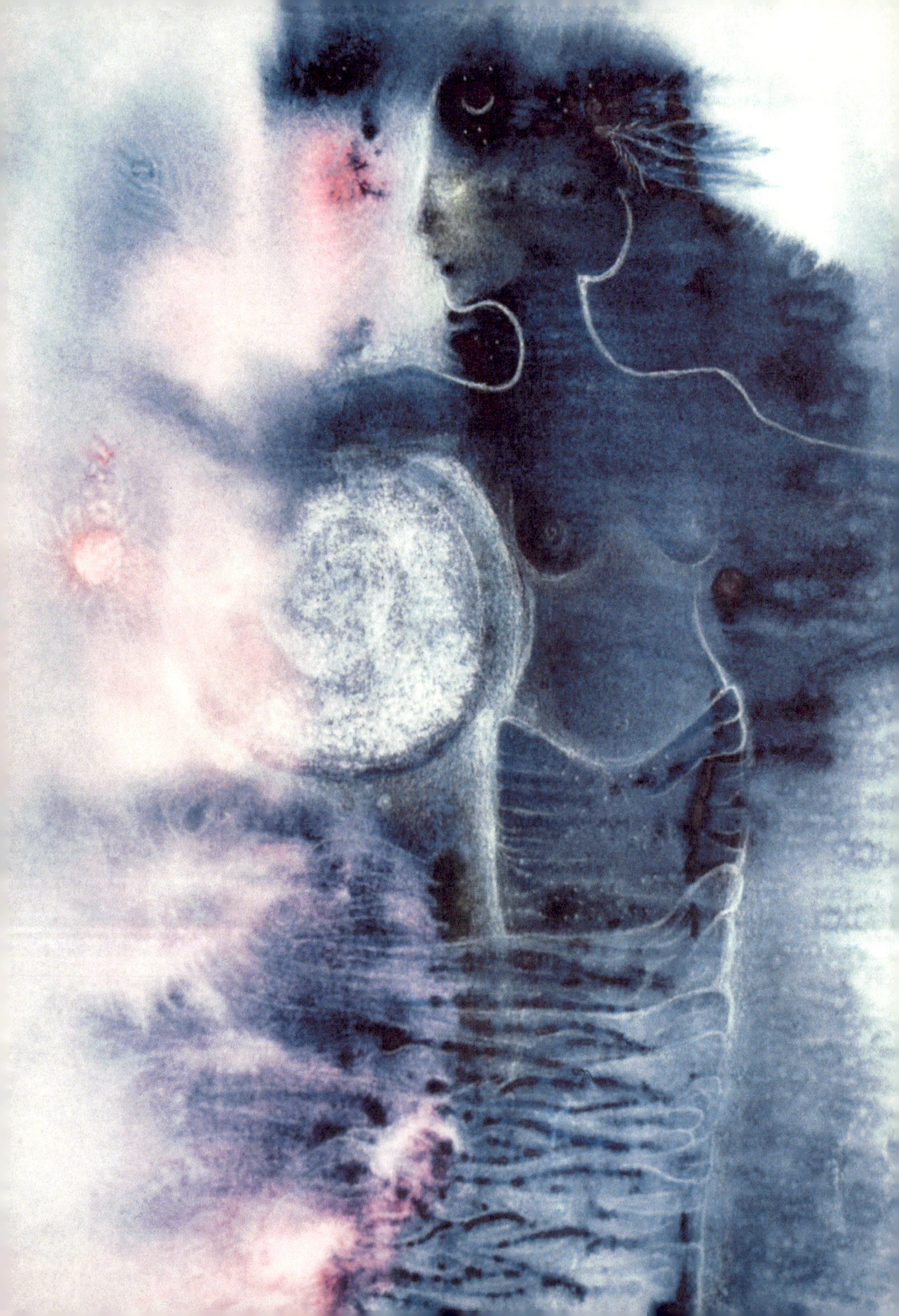

SHE…of the Universe

The One does spiral in…
announcing self as form…
The formless it does stay…
dancing in time…
refolding…
disappearing…
knowing time as naught…

Divine feminine here dances the play
of Creator as Creation and back again to zero.
The universe as one verse of poetic resounding.
Let us play.

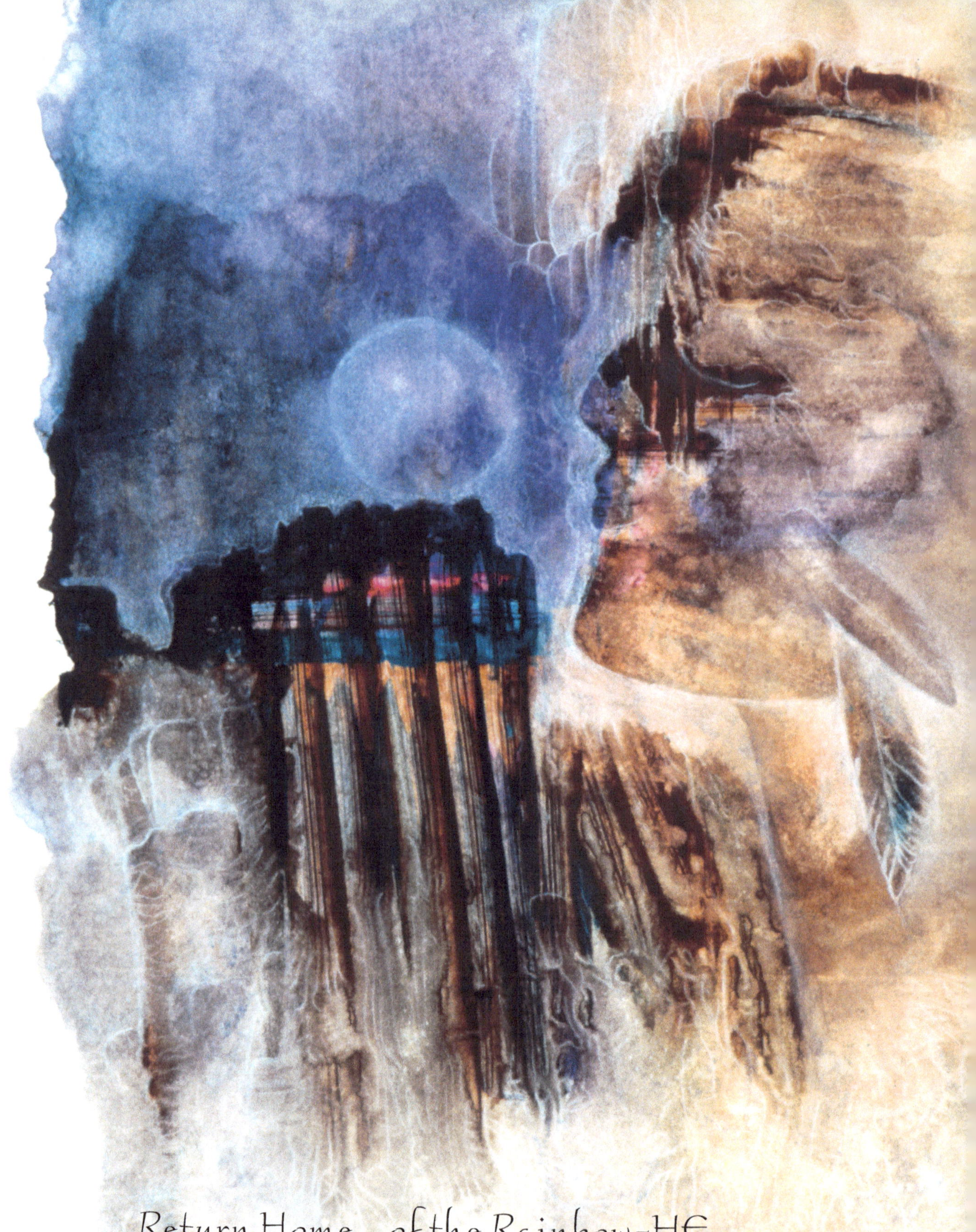

Return Home...of the Rainbow-HE

Return Home...of the Rainbow-HE...
to the mesa...of the SHE...
on the night...of the rising moon...

This painting conveys the sacred union of seeming opposites.

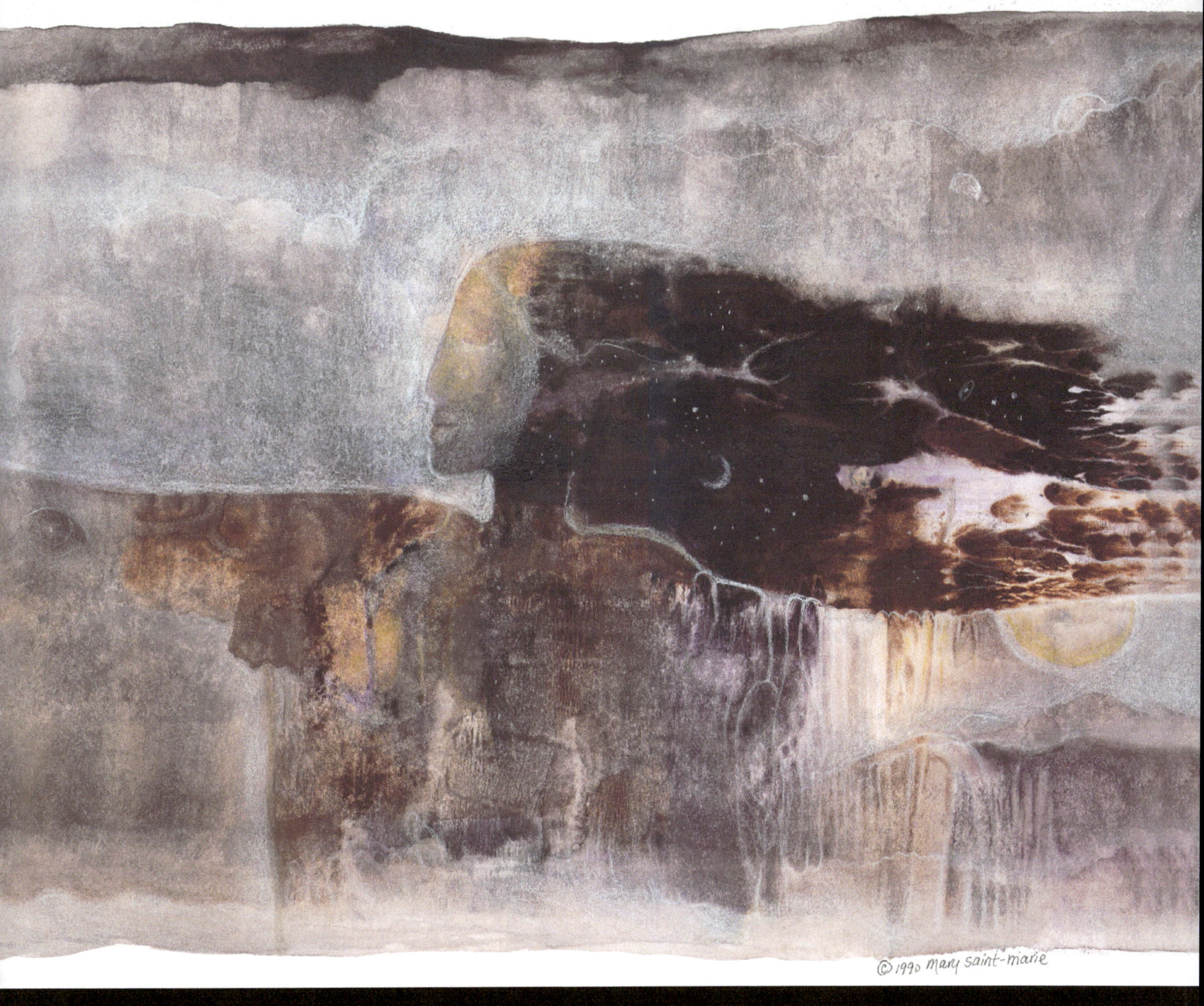

Journey-He...from the Stars unto the Stones

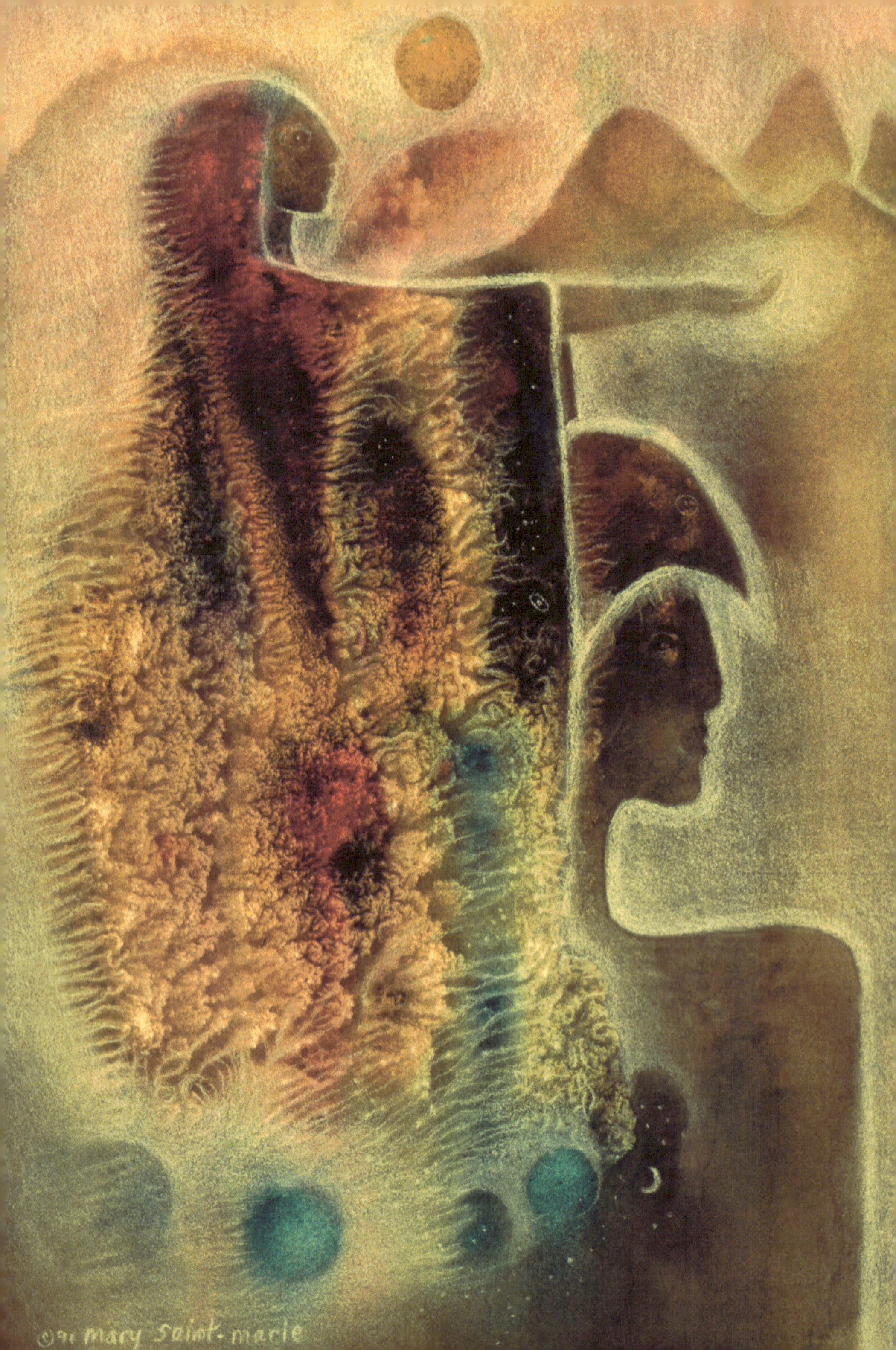
©91 mary saint-marie

The Rainbow Gift

Approaching now
goddess of reciprocity…
living in his heart…

HE comes…
bearing The Rainbow Gift…

This painting calls forth the Law of Love, that is,
the great law of giving and equal regiving.
It calls forth the understanding that inviolate is this
Law of Balance in all the universe.

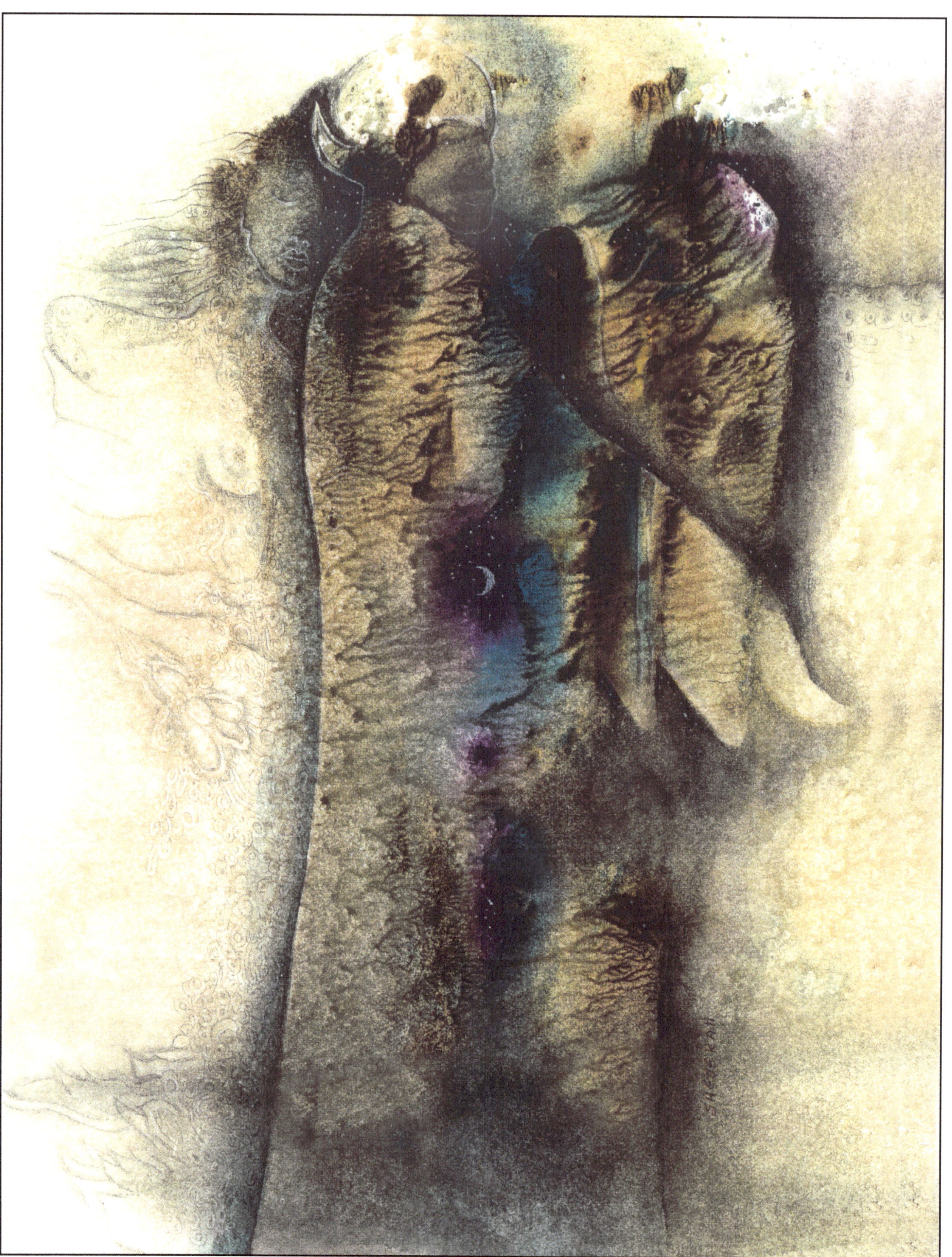

Ceremony of the Gift

This is an ancient call...
It is The Call...
A call heard deep in every heart...
It is the call to give...
In that...is the regiving...
and balance is reclaimed...

Ceremony of the Gift is a remembrance of our need to give.
It is a remembrance that we all are shamans,
giving forth from the mystery. And indeed, it is not even our gift.
Only our gift to give. It is a primordial need.
For when we give the Gift....
we touch the place...where we know the other One.

SHE and HE...together give the gift.
Together...they remember the ceremony of the gift.

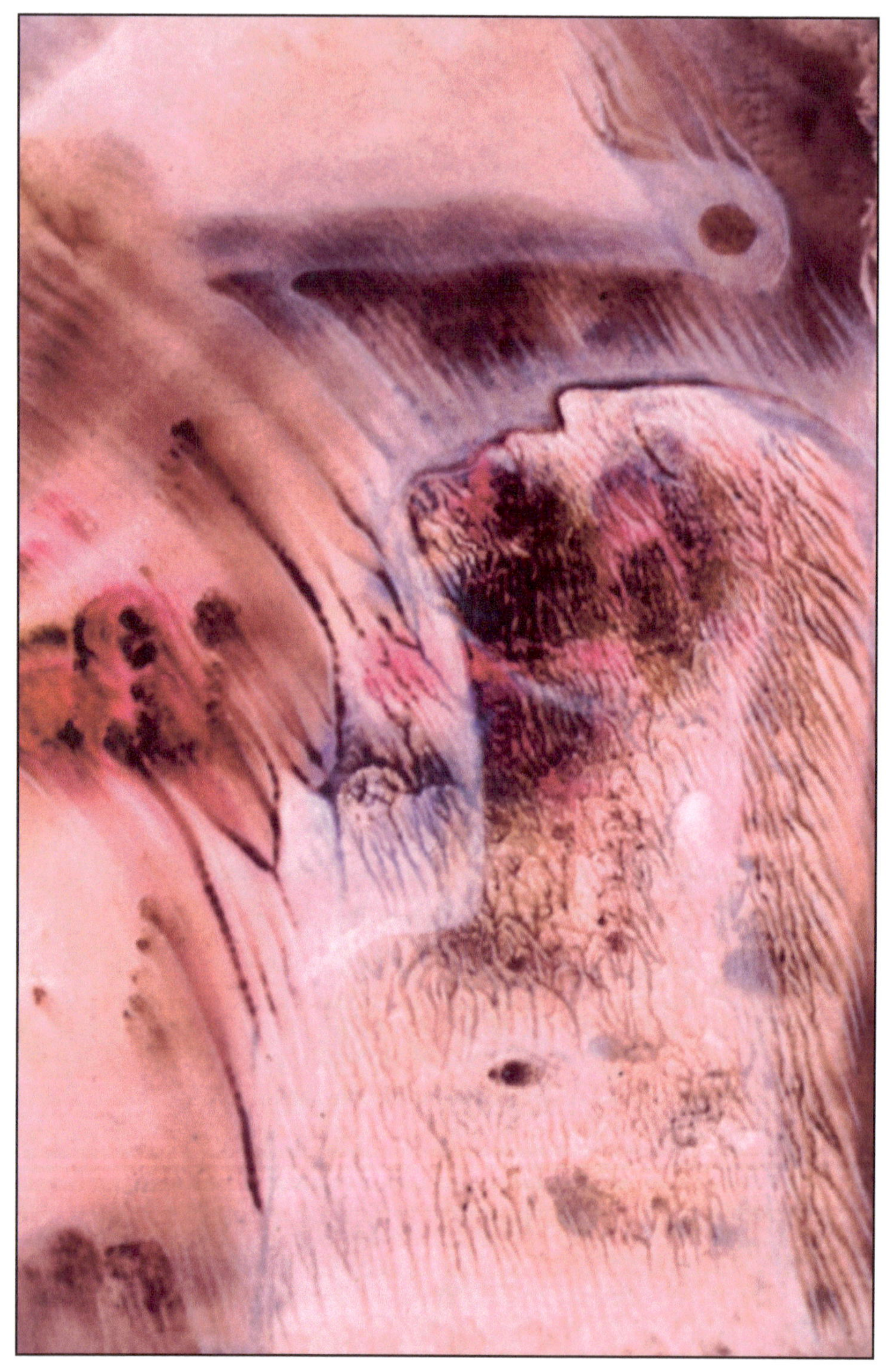

Ancient-Beauty-HE...it is...

Ancient-Beauty-HE...it is...
who comes and soars...as does the eagle...

True and archetypal man does merge with the trees, the flowers, the sky...that is.
HE finds his peace in the single eye and takes flight in the One...

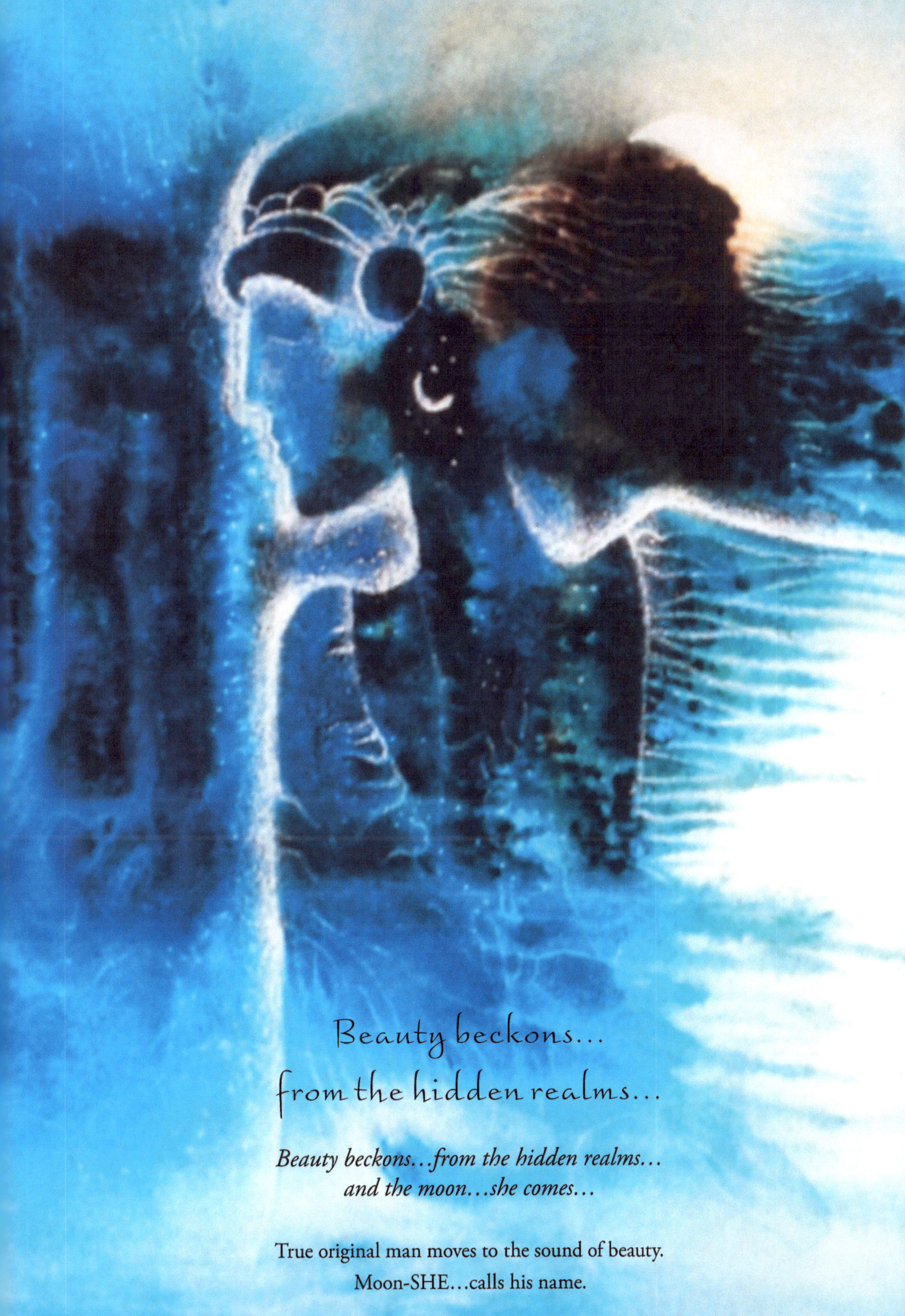

Beauty beckons…
from the hidden realms…

Beauty beckons…from the hidden realms…
and the moon…she comes…

True original man moves to the sound of beauty.
Moon-SHE…calls his name.

Ceremony of the Midnight Sun

with ancient staff flaming...
primal Mask of Heaven...
does walk this very earth...
as shaman...

HE...does know...
that child-like wonder
does fill his very days...

and lo...do form and formless...
merge as One...
in Ceremony...of the Midnight Sun...

This painting is a revelation of the child-like wonder
that is the very essence of shaman-healer-sage.
Here medicine man emerges as one of dove-like peace
ever borne in one who loves.

Here the ancient flaming staff stands glowing
as symbol of ancient caduceus
and symbol of the masculine principle.
And midnight sun serves as the symbol
of the moon-divine feminine principle.
In shaman...they live as Balance...
the union of HE and SHE...

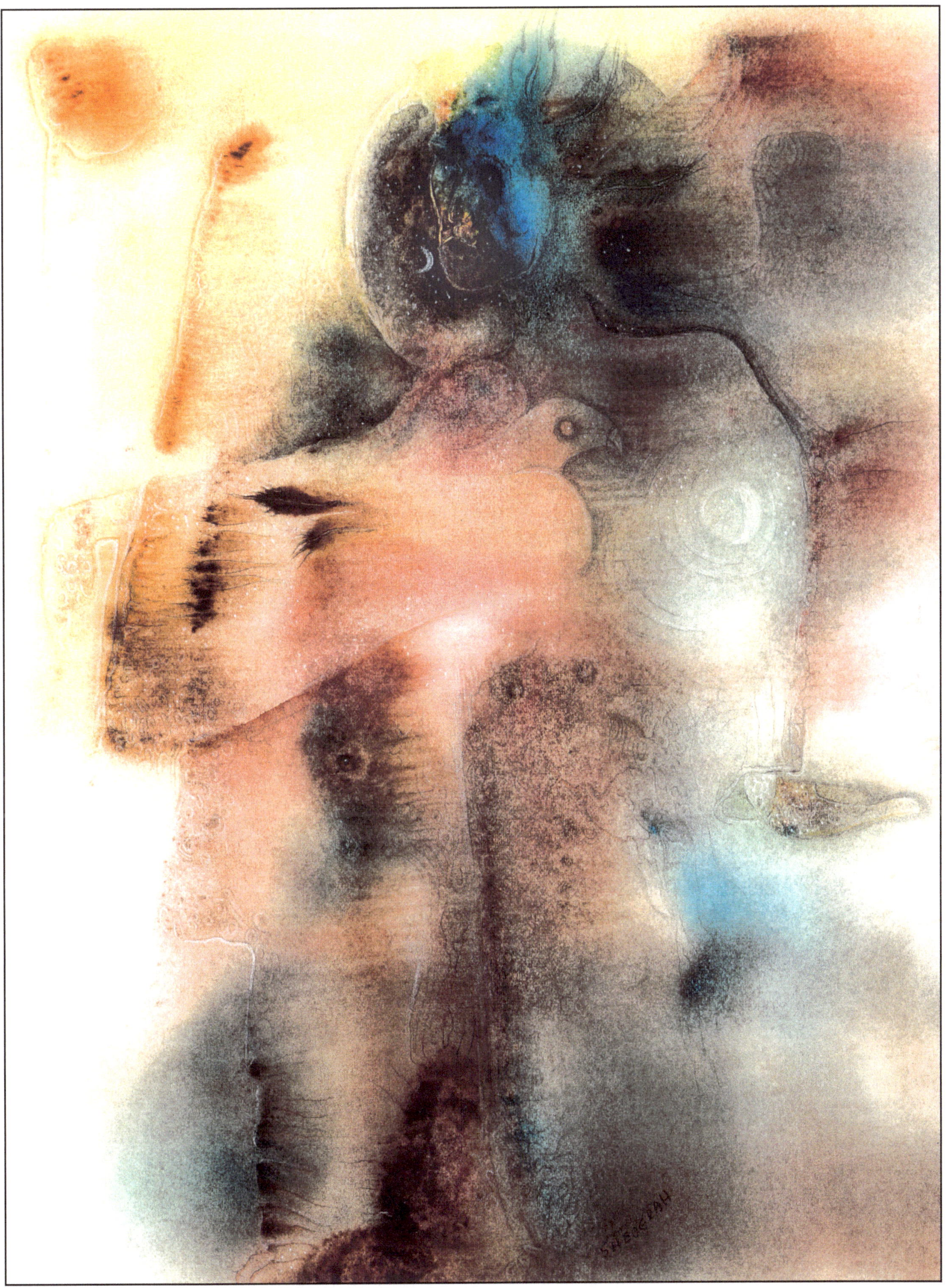

Eagle Calls...

Eagle Calls...
I fly...
high above the
madding crowd...
and I see...

Clear vision is revealed
as expansion of consciousness.
It is revealed as sight of single
eye, dwelling ever within...

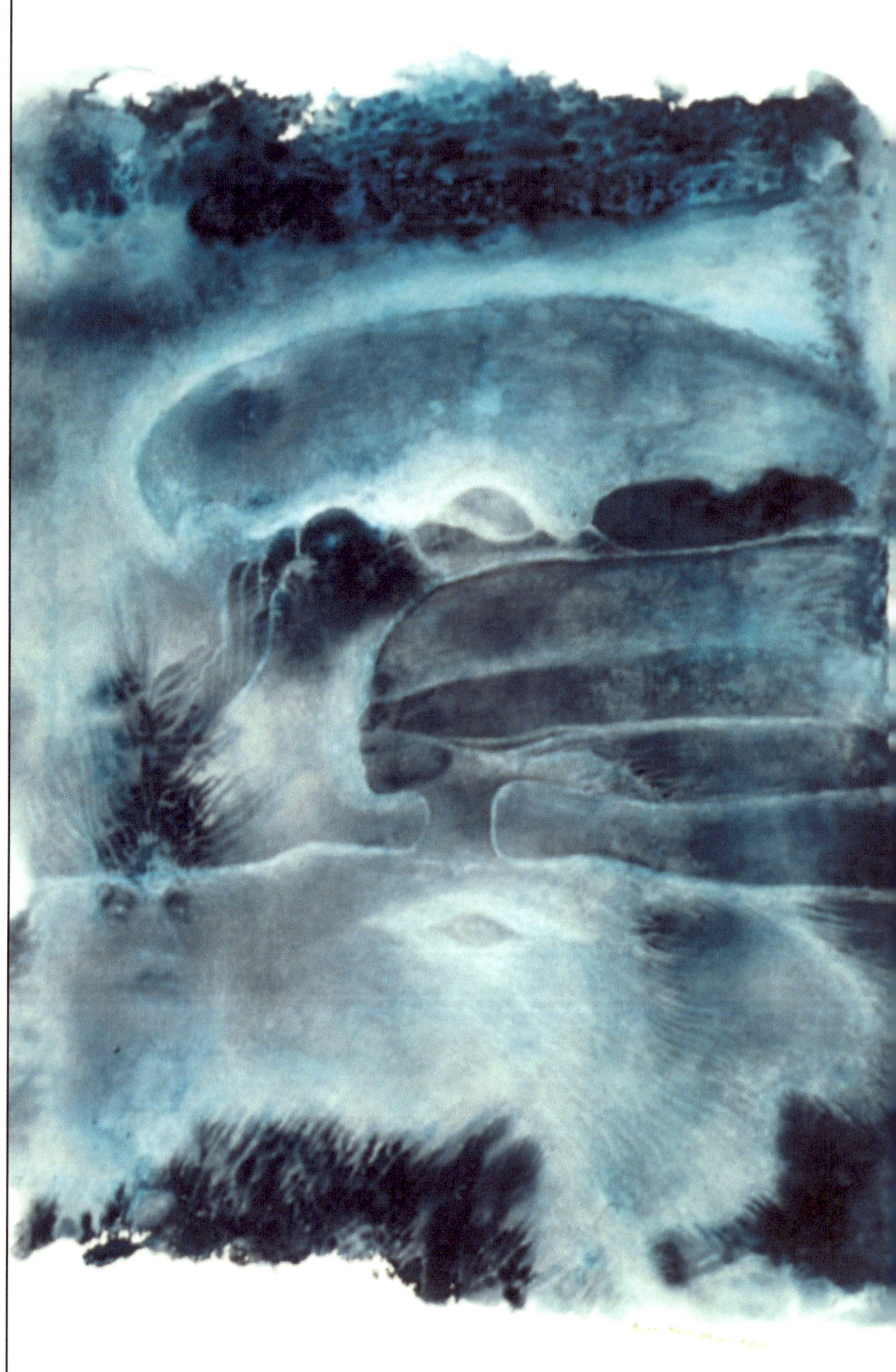

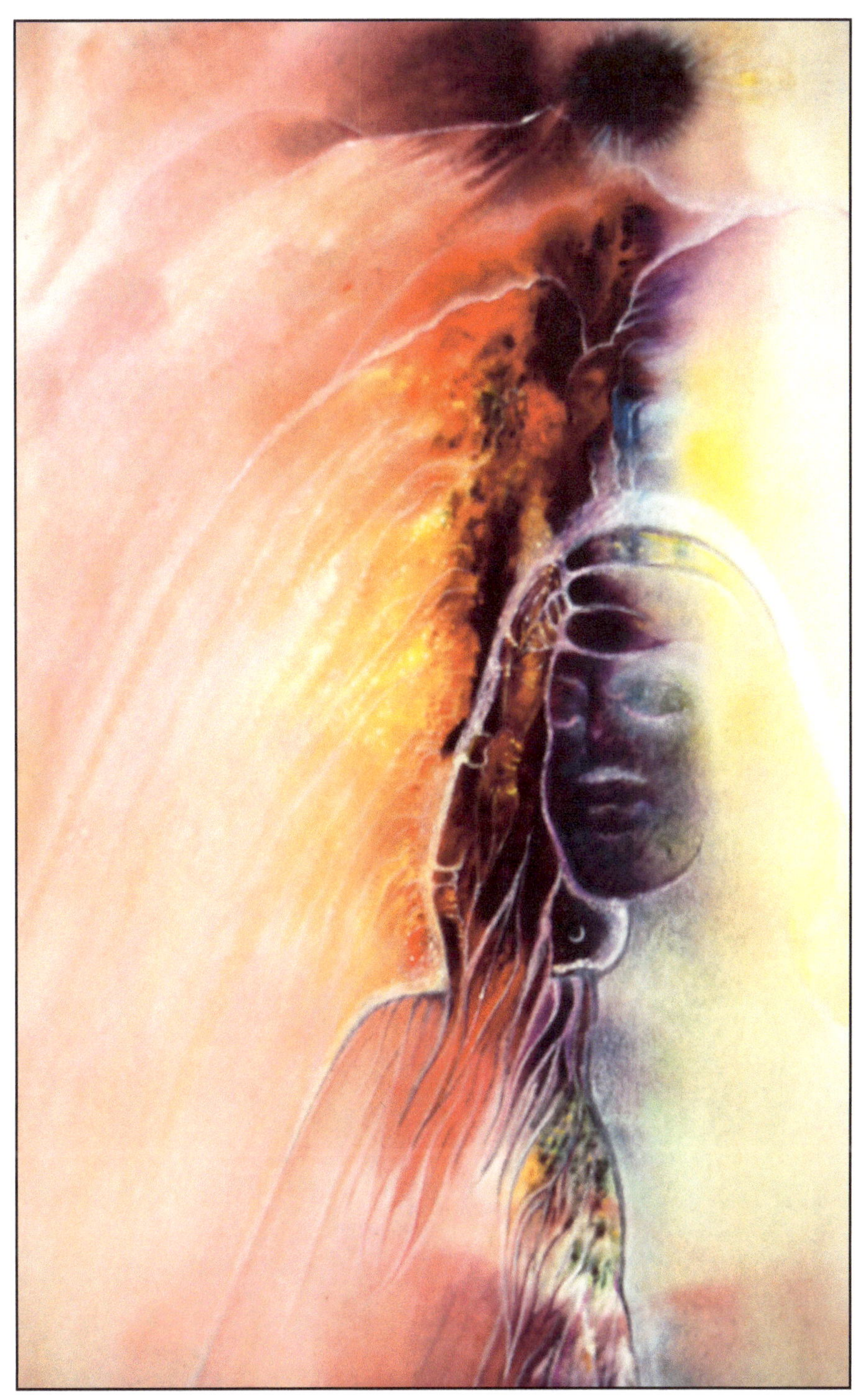

Infinity's Rainbow Dance

Infinity's Rainbow Dance of Oneness…
does fill the earth…
and fill the sky…

True man is here in the realization of the One as the Many…

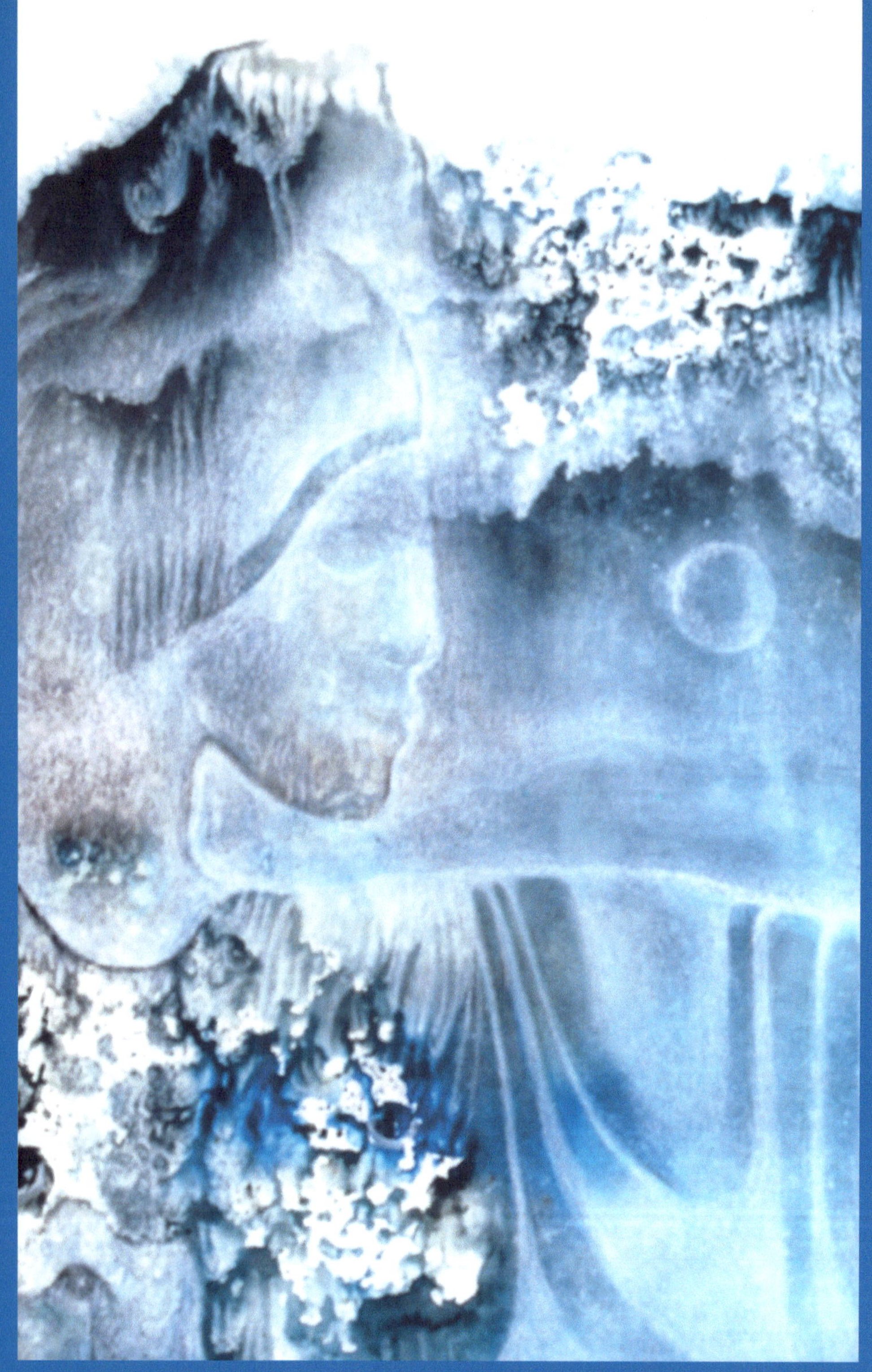

Peace...Peace at Last

Peace appears...
in the SHE...of all Creation...
and battle...
it is done...

Man is robed in the blue of the feminine principle of creation. The receptive is the Bringer of Peace.

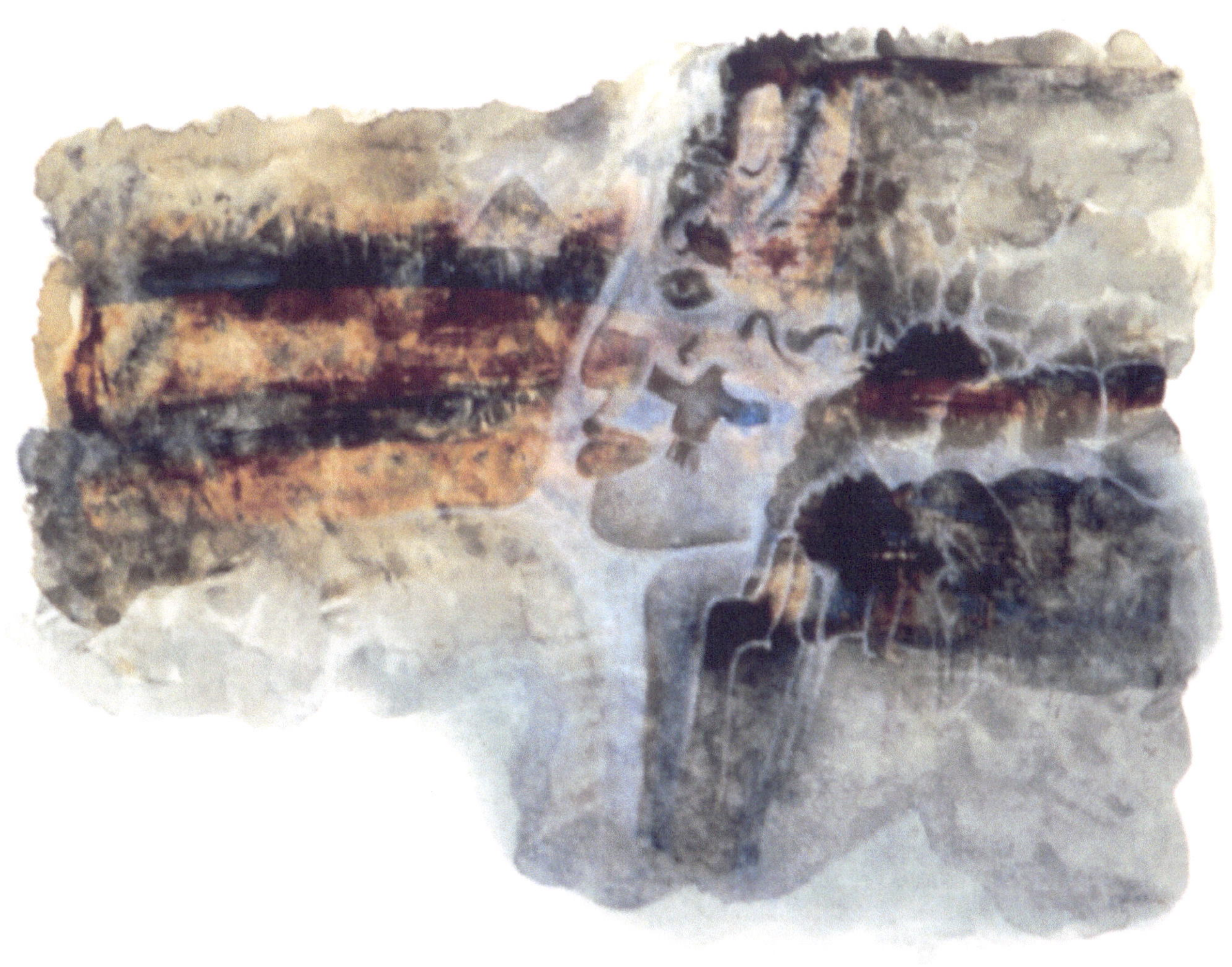

HE…of the Rocks

Primal-HE…of the rocks…
bird, snake, lizard…
dwelling in his mind…

That the world is within is represented here with petroglyphs of the mind…

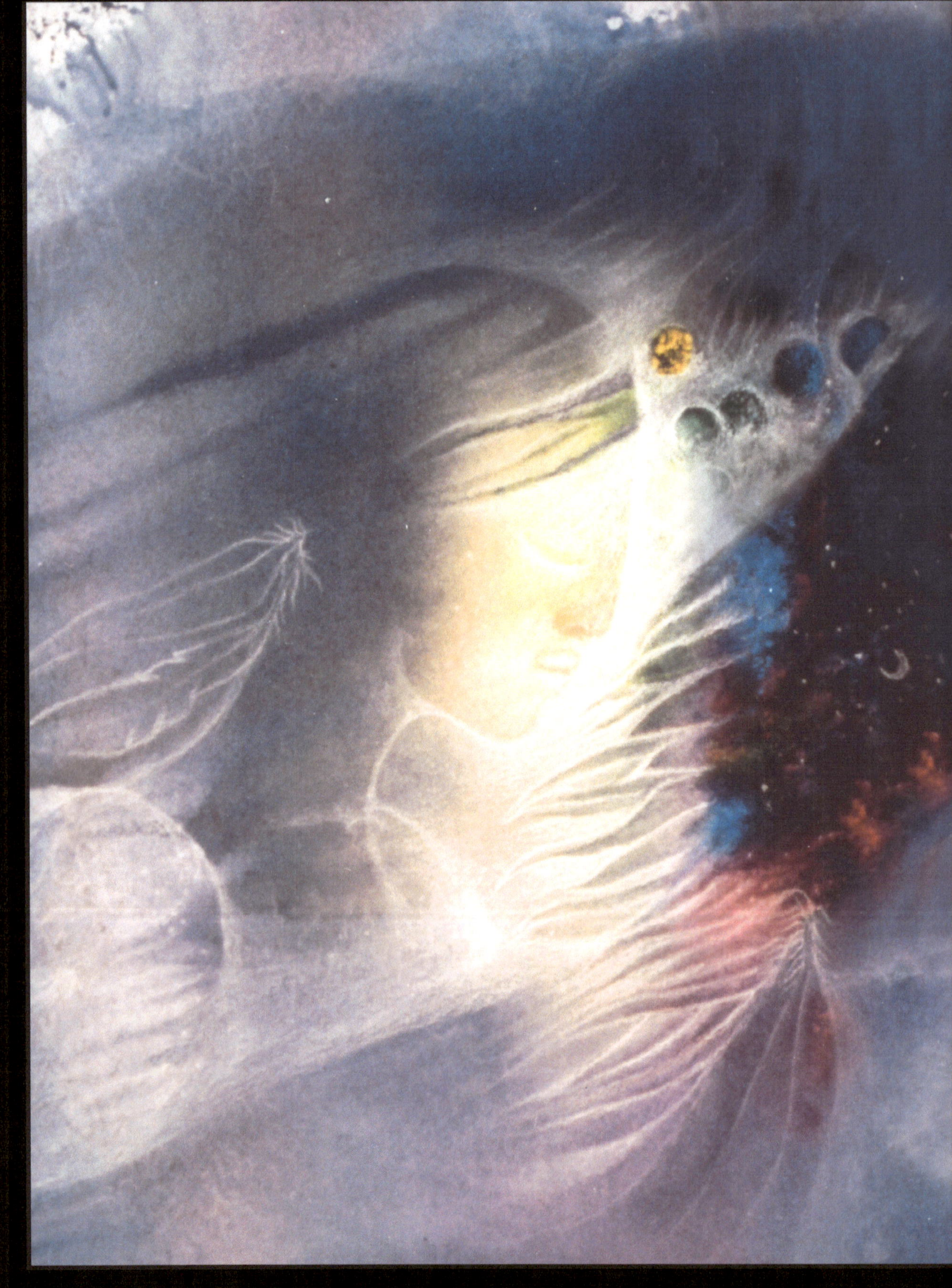

Sky-dancer-HE

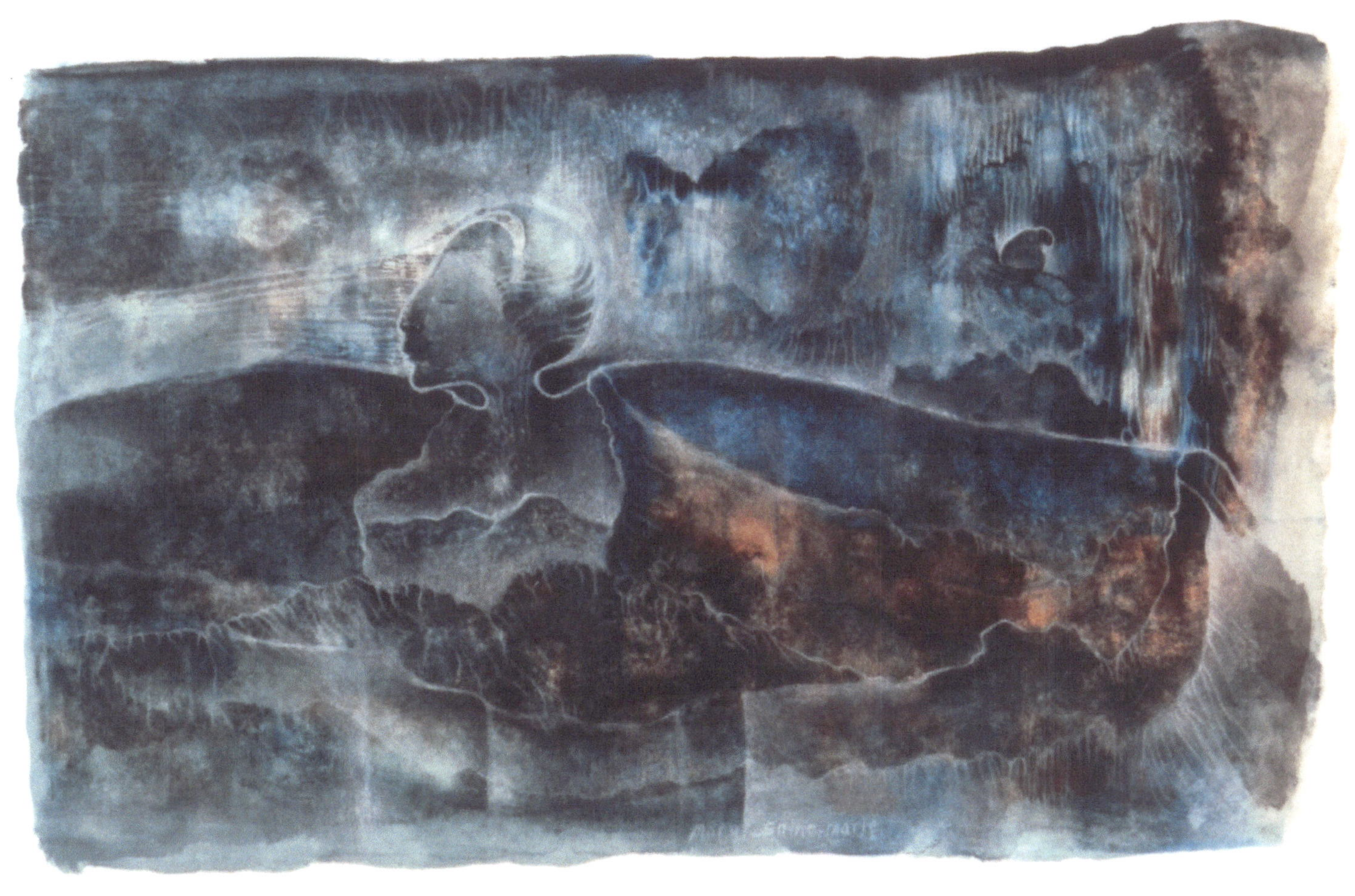

Beauty-HE...awaits...

Beauty-HE...awaits...
in the cave...
of the holy of holies...

Man does open wide his heart and SHE...appears.
This painting is a symbol of the within...appearing outwardly.

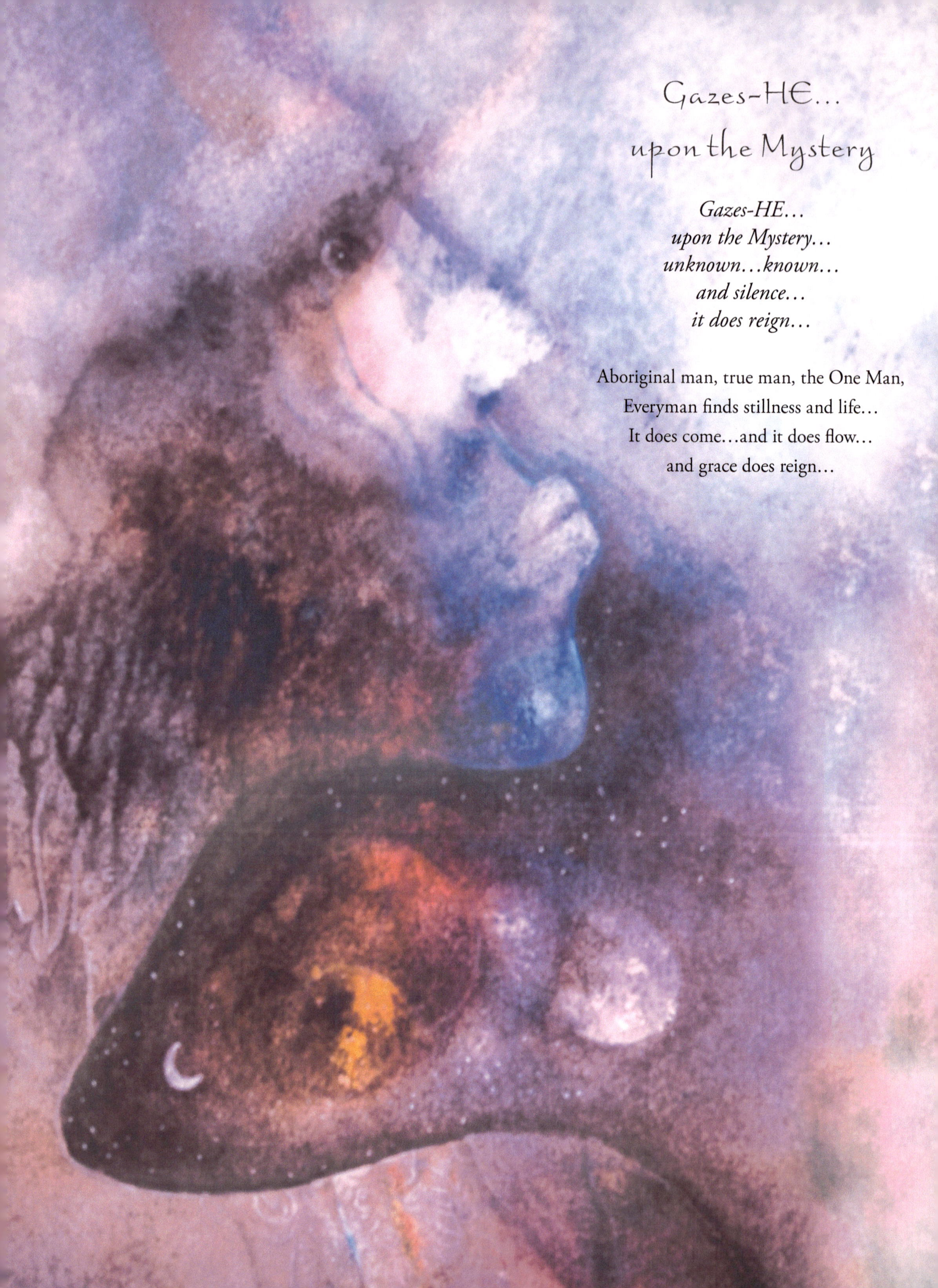

Gazes-HE...
upon the Mystery

Gazes-HE...
upon the Mystery...
unknown...known...
and silence...
it does reign...

Aboriginal man, true man, the One Man,
Everyman finds stillness and life...
It does come...and it does flow...
and grace does reign...

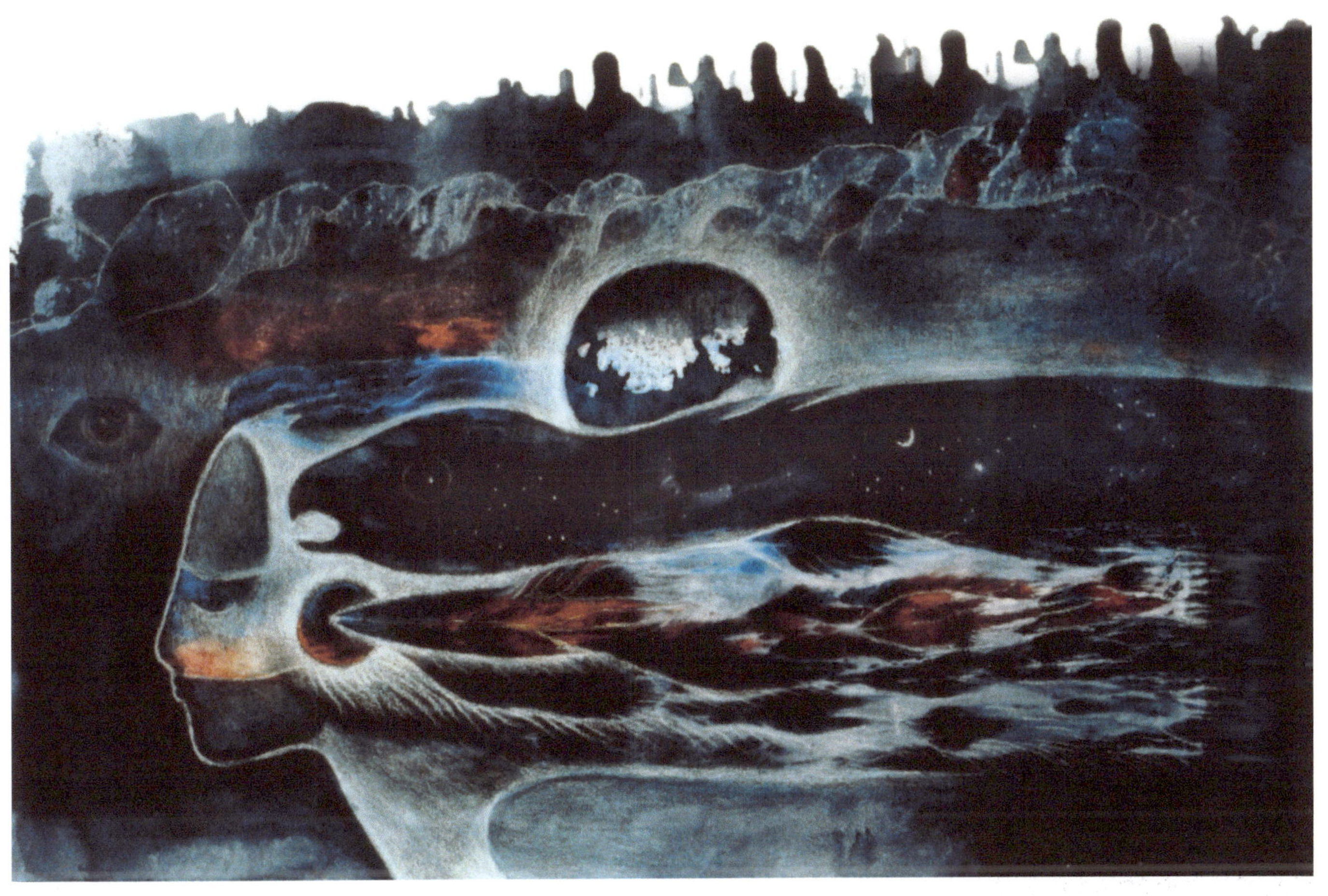

Native-HE...dances with birds

Native-HE...dances with birds...
and flies over the glowing lands...

Interconnectedness and interrelatedness are felt here as the illumined tapestry that is Life.

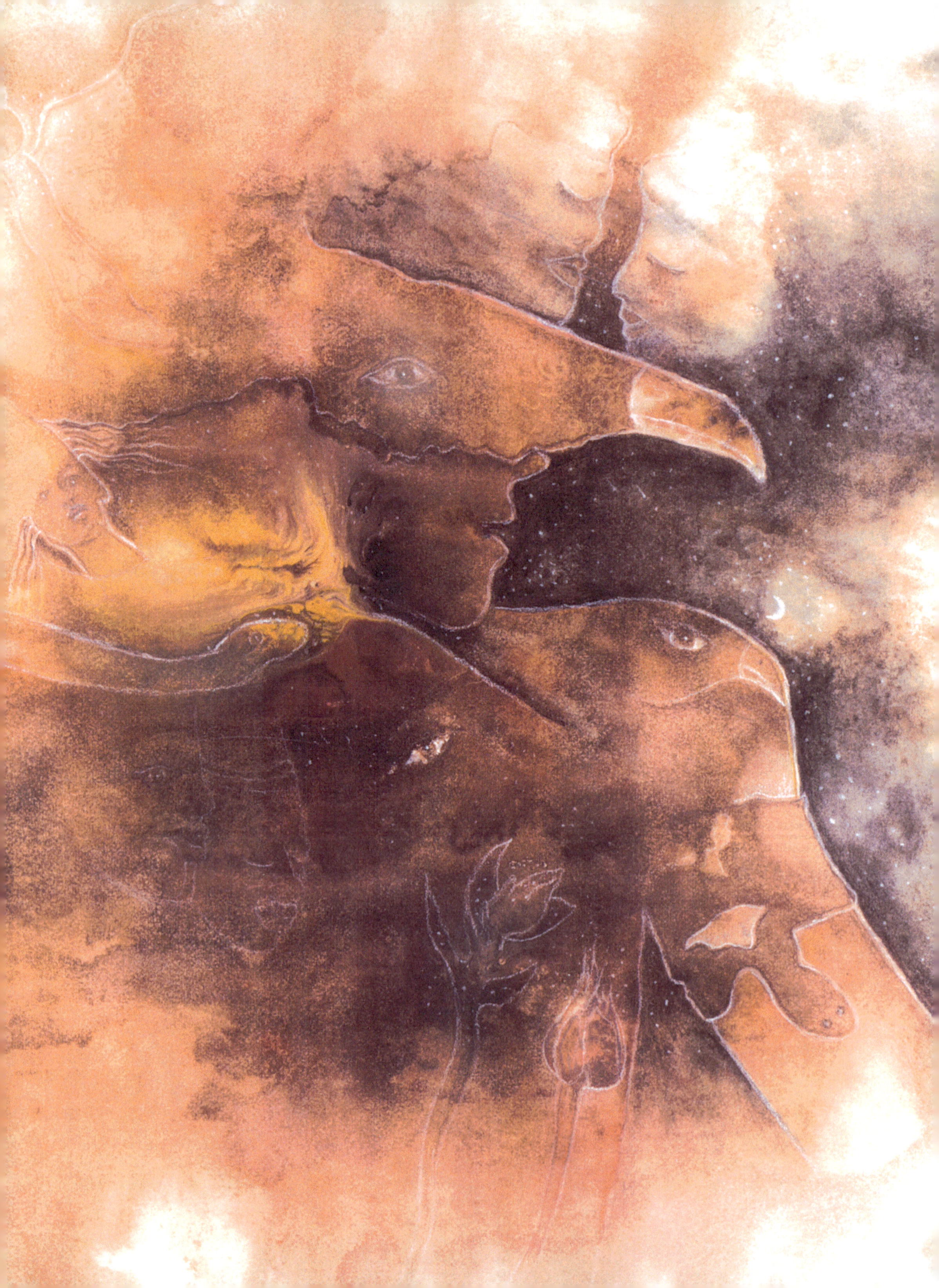

Shapeshifter-HE

HE can feel Her…pouring…spilling from his heart…
He can feel Her…dancing at Infinity's door…
Trembling…She emerges…
The serpents-dance…it comes…

Man, in this image, has shapeshifted with bird and taken flight.
The flight is in consciousness and another world is seen.
It is a world where balance reigns.
A world where Oneness dances, lives and breathes.
A wild freedom…It does come…

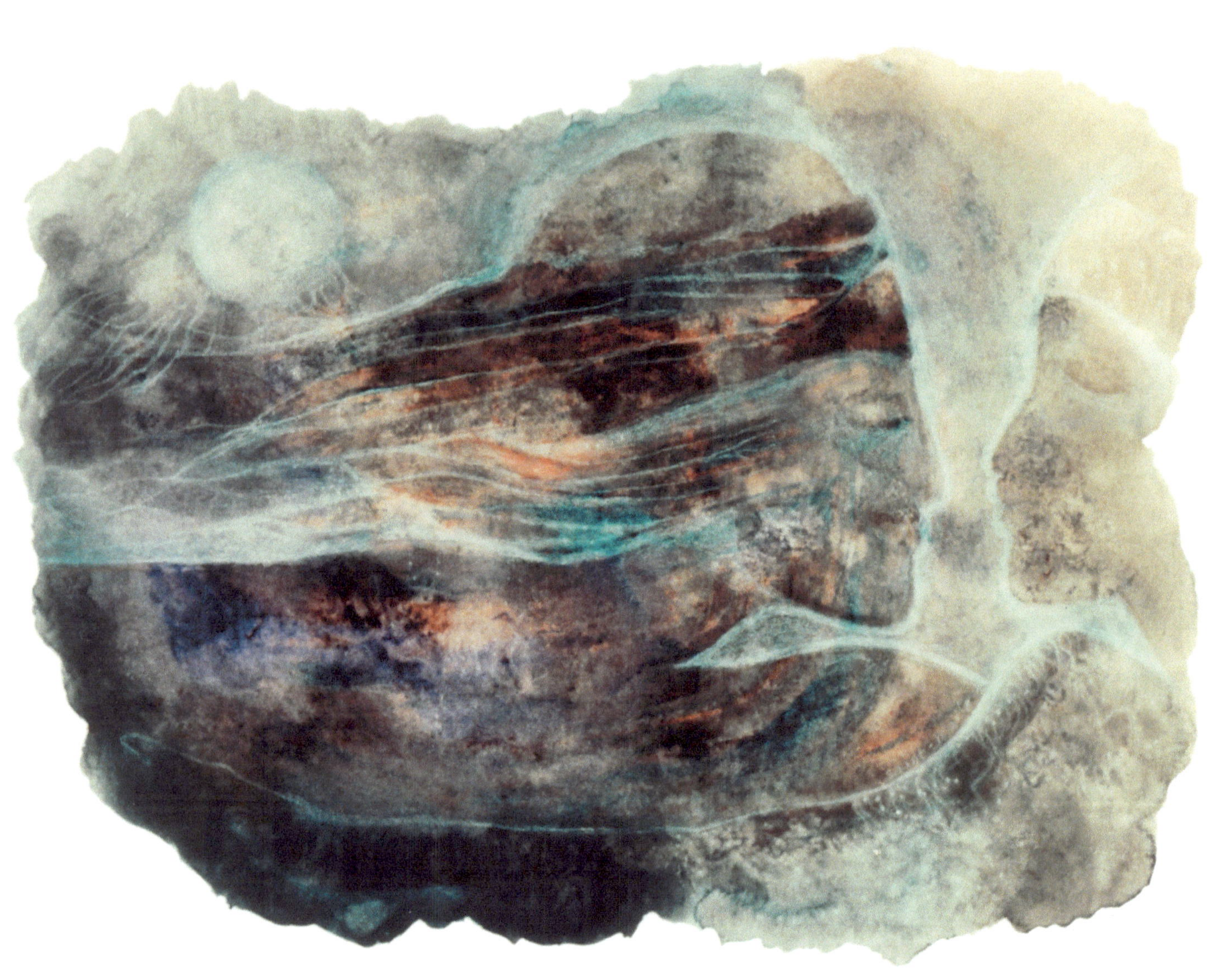

Rainbow-HE

Rainbow-HE…does dwell
in the ever present light of knowing…

Rainbow-HE is the one who finds the vast withiness and SHE does come.
The One within…the One without.

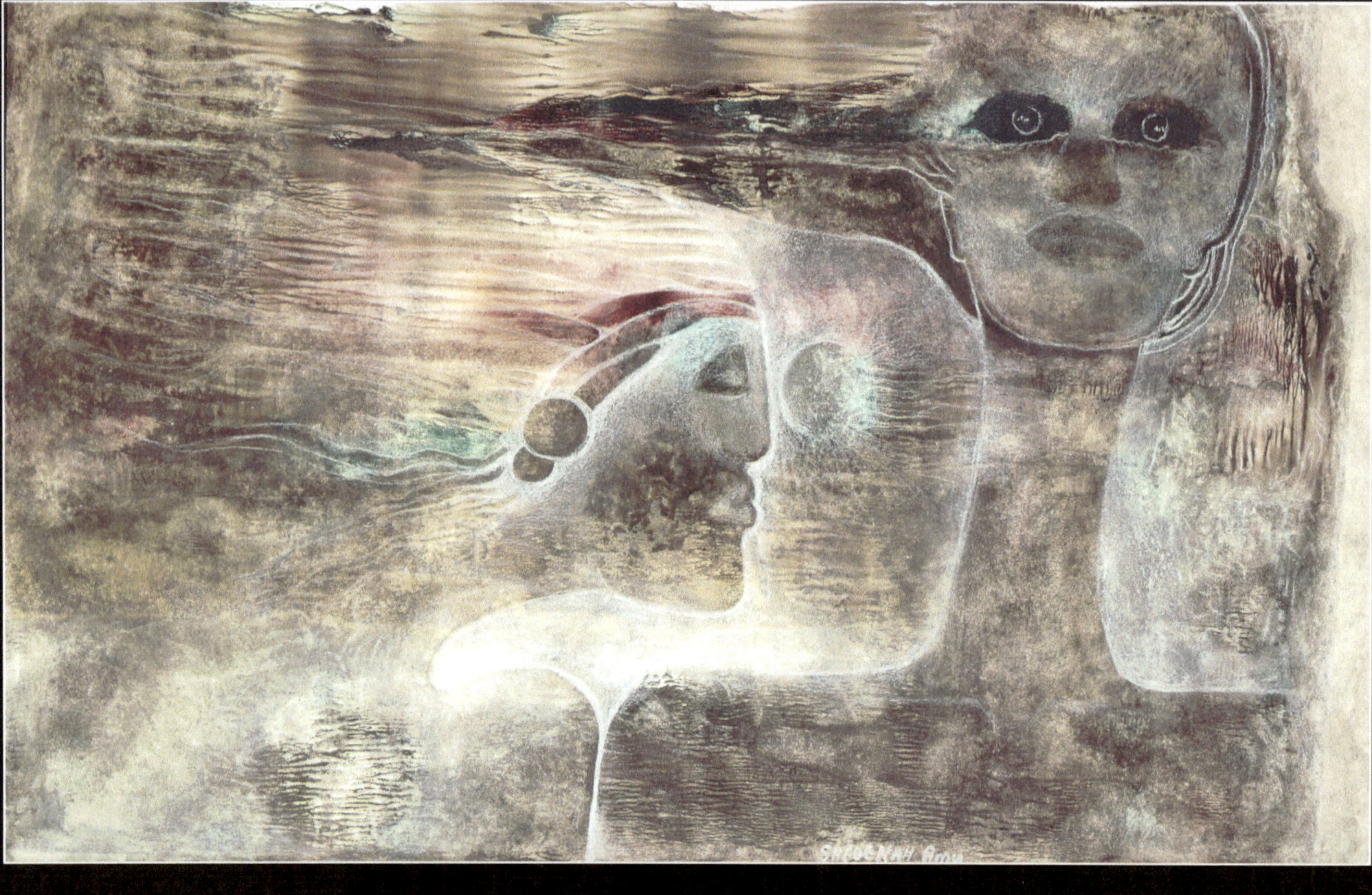

Sacred Merging of the Kachina Mystery

HE and SHE…do come…
as two…they do appear…

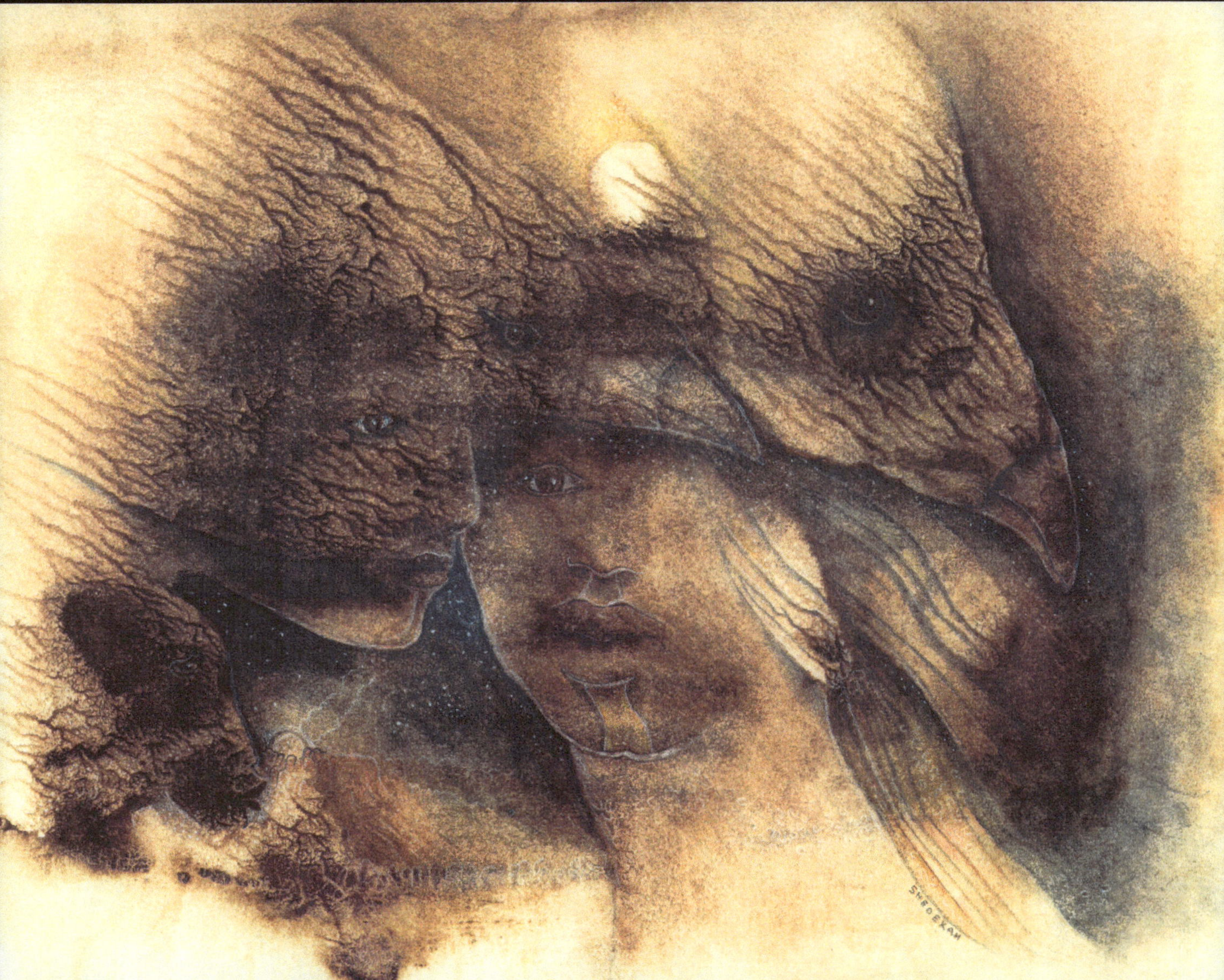

The Ancient Ones

The Ancient Ones…they watch…
they wait…they know…
and they stay silent…

And whispers come…from in the rocks…
and…they hear…

The Ancient Ones touches that place in the silence where "Knowing" awaits our coming. It ever calls that we might hear. That we might hear the speaking from the silent rocks, from the silent spaces in time, from the silent realm that dwells within our soul.

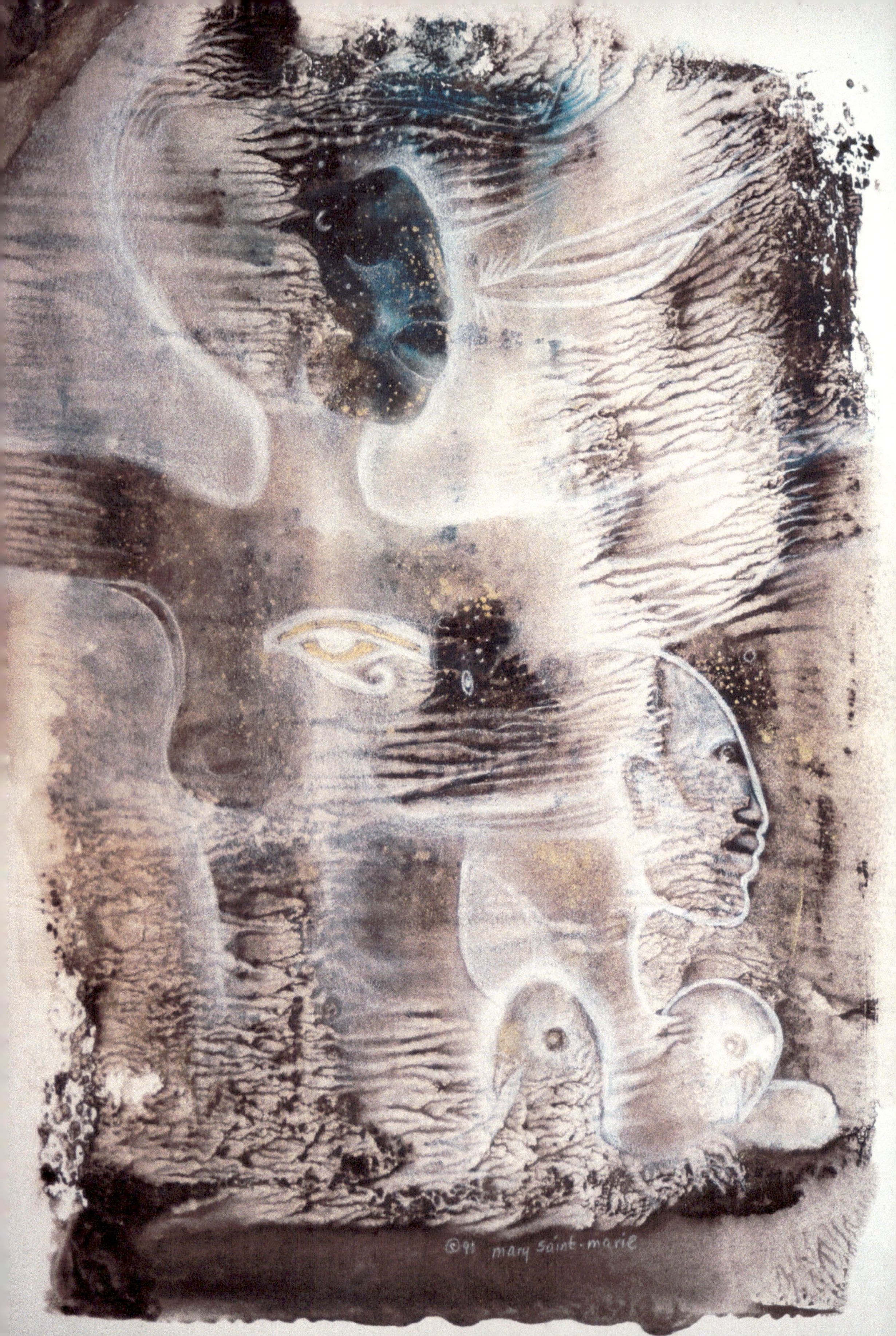
mary saint-marie

Beauty-SHE and HE...
embraced by the Universe...

Beauty-SHE and HE...
embraced by the Universe...

And full they are...
with stars and moons...
reflections of the world within...

That the world is within comes as a fearless thought.
Truth stands naked before us...a single eye...
Fear does fall away.
We are embraced by the ever present spiritual universe.
Let us drink of this vision...

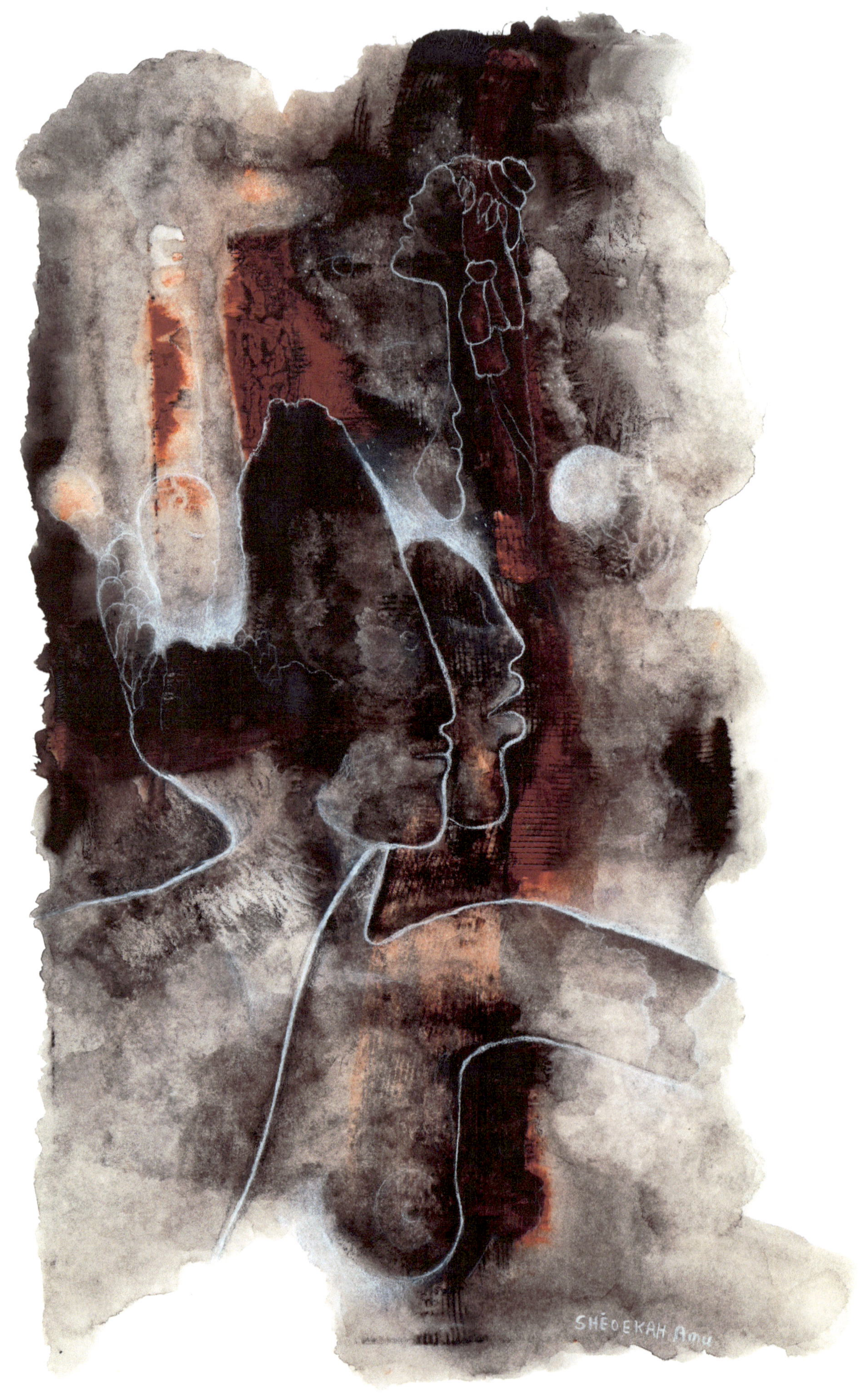
SHĔDEKAH Amu

and together...
they dream and sing...

and together...they dream
and sing of worlds unseen...
and together...they build...
the royal twos...they build...

and the tribes...they land...
in the sacred two by twos...

they know well...
and they Remember...

Imaged here is the Unmanifest One...manifest as The Sacred Two.
Imaged here is the sacredness of that holy union.

Behold-SHE

SHE does sit among the stars...
and SHE...does see the world...
The world...SHE knows...
doth dwell within...

It mirrors forth...and lo...
Creation does seem to lie...
before our very eyes...

This painting reveals that the world lies within our Consciousness...
and it is an invitation to find that place where all are One...

This painting is of a masked-SHE...under which is this precious Universe...
Behold...

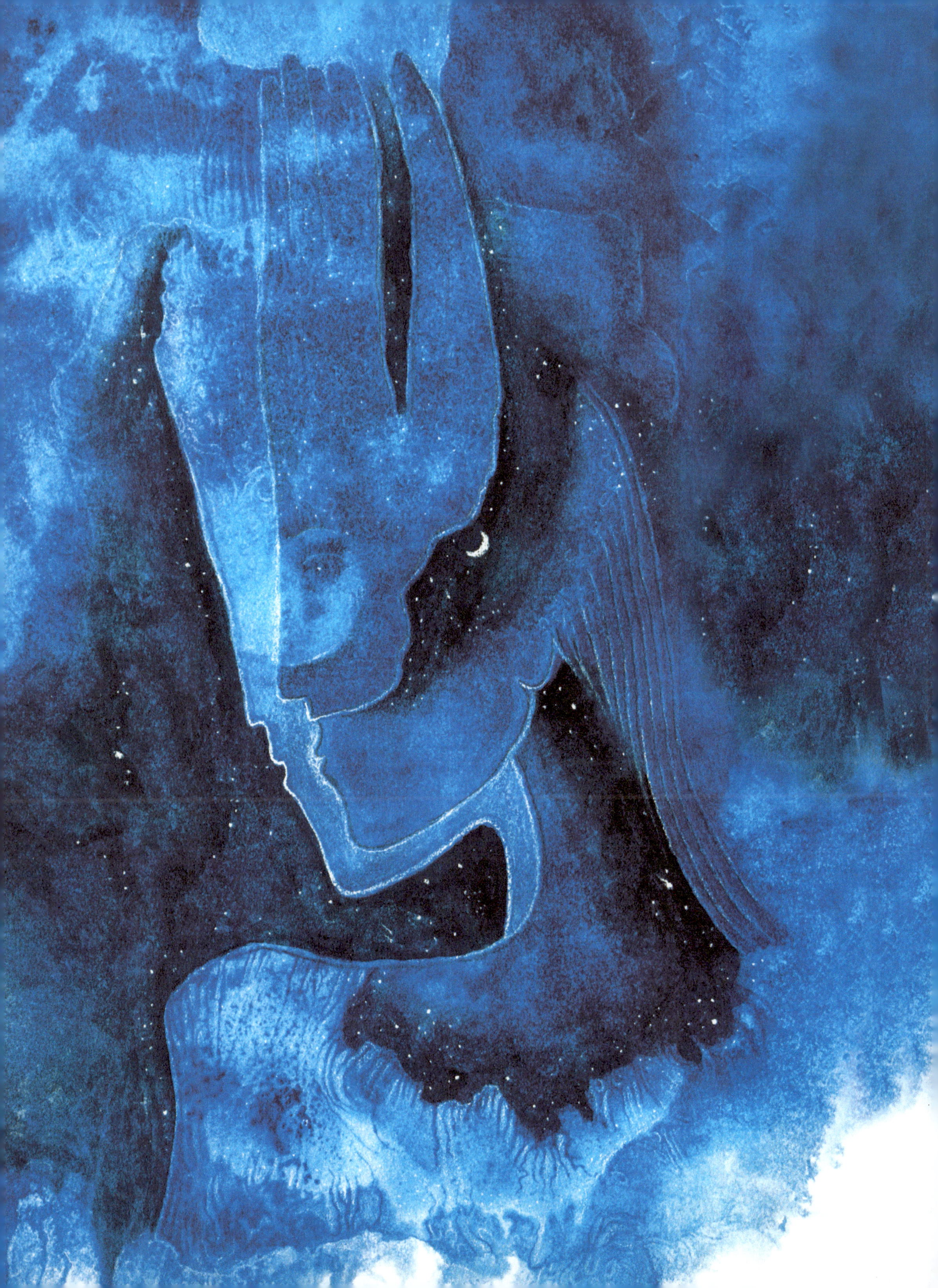

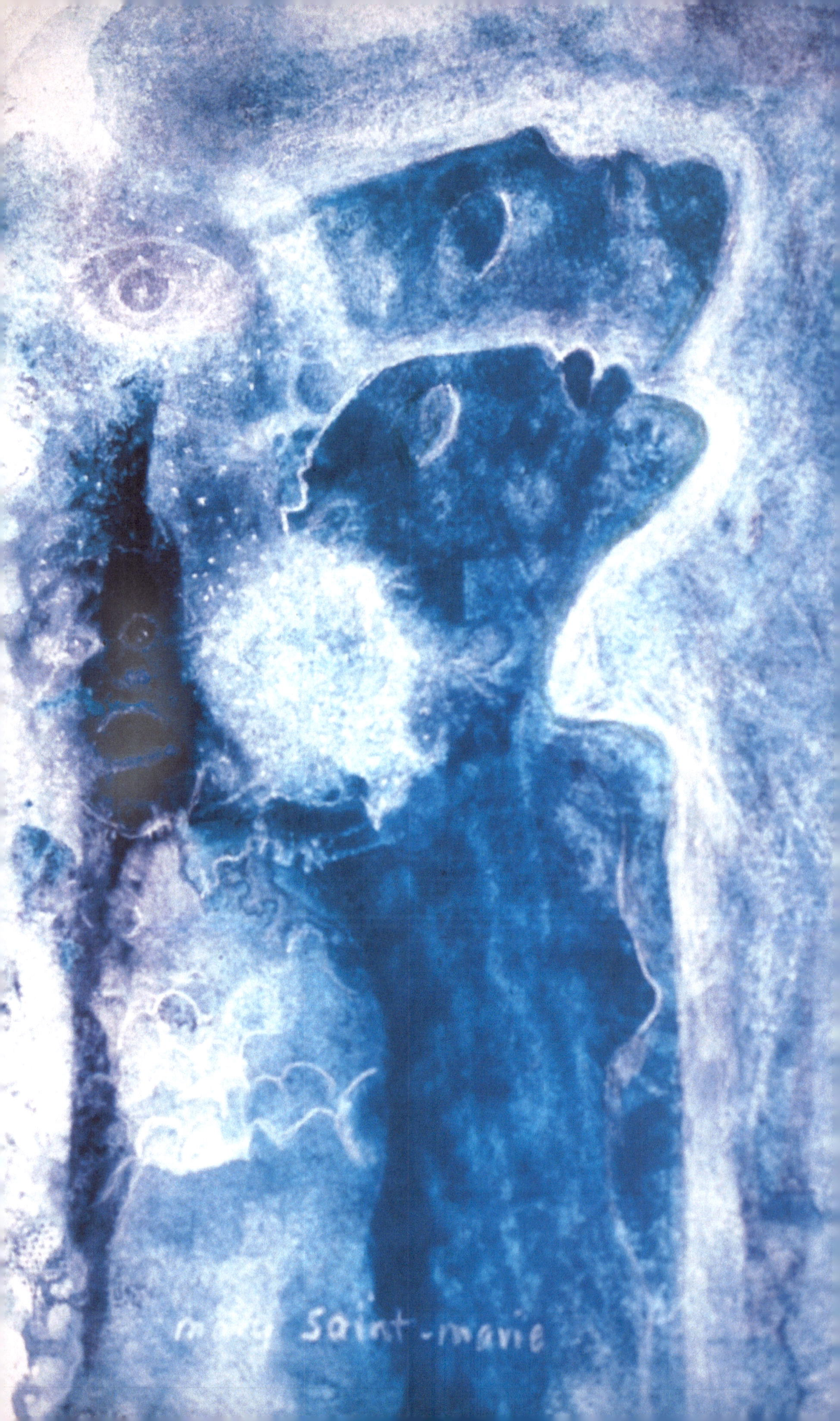

Saint-marie

In Grand Silence comes forth the Child

Primal...HE and SHE...
hearken to another world...

Silence speaks...
and is borne the child of joy...

Original man and woman do hear the call...beyond the world where ears do listen. Borne of this union is the child named joy...borne of the incorporeal.

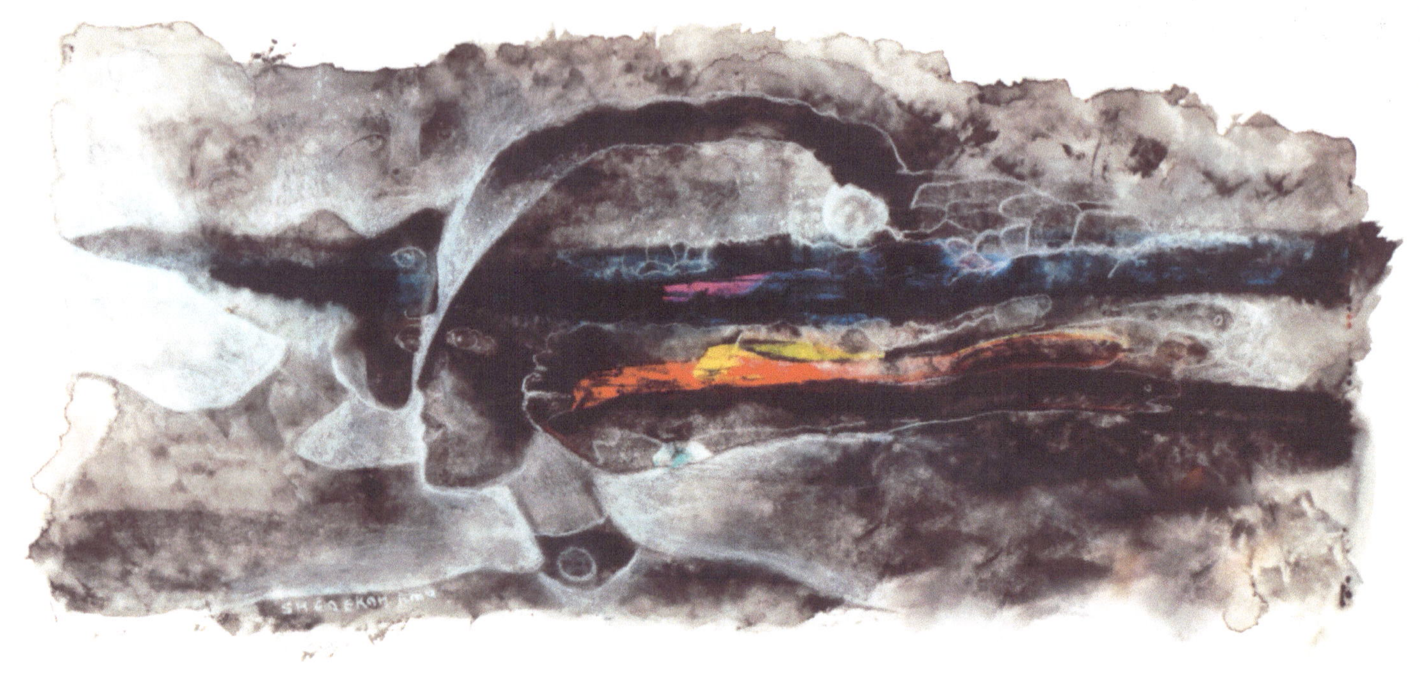

Shapeshifter-HE and SHE

HE and SHE…as the mountains…

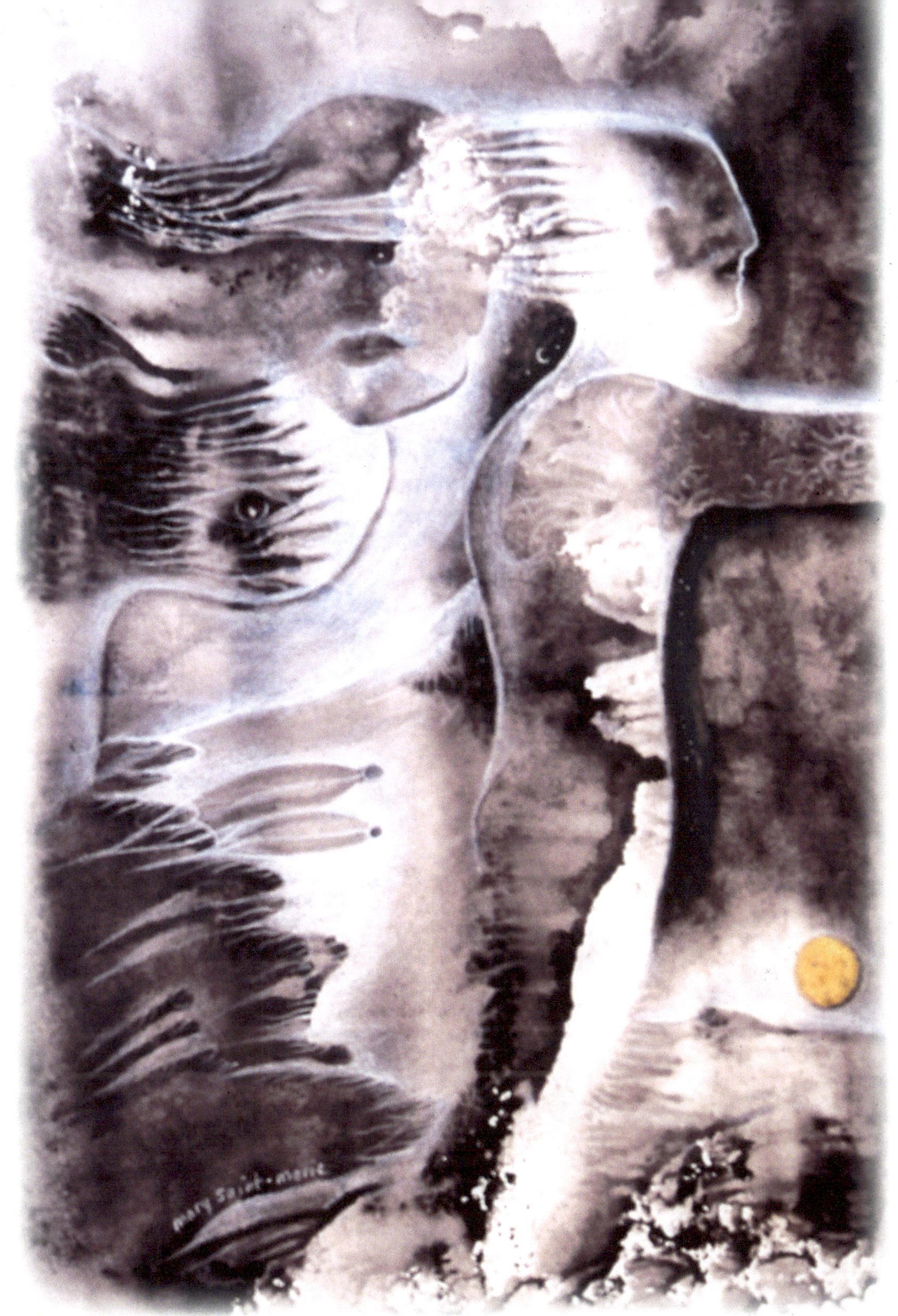

O Wind I Am

O Wind I Am…
and the rising moon…
and SHE…

Revealed here is wind, man and woman as One.

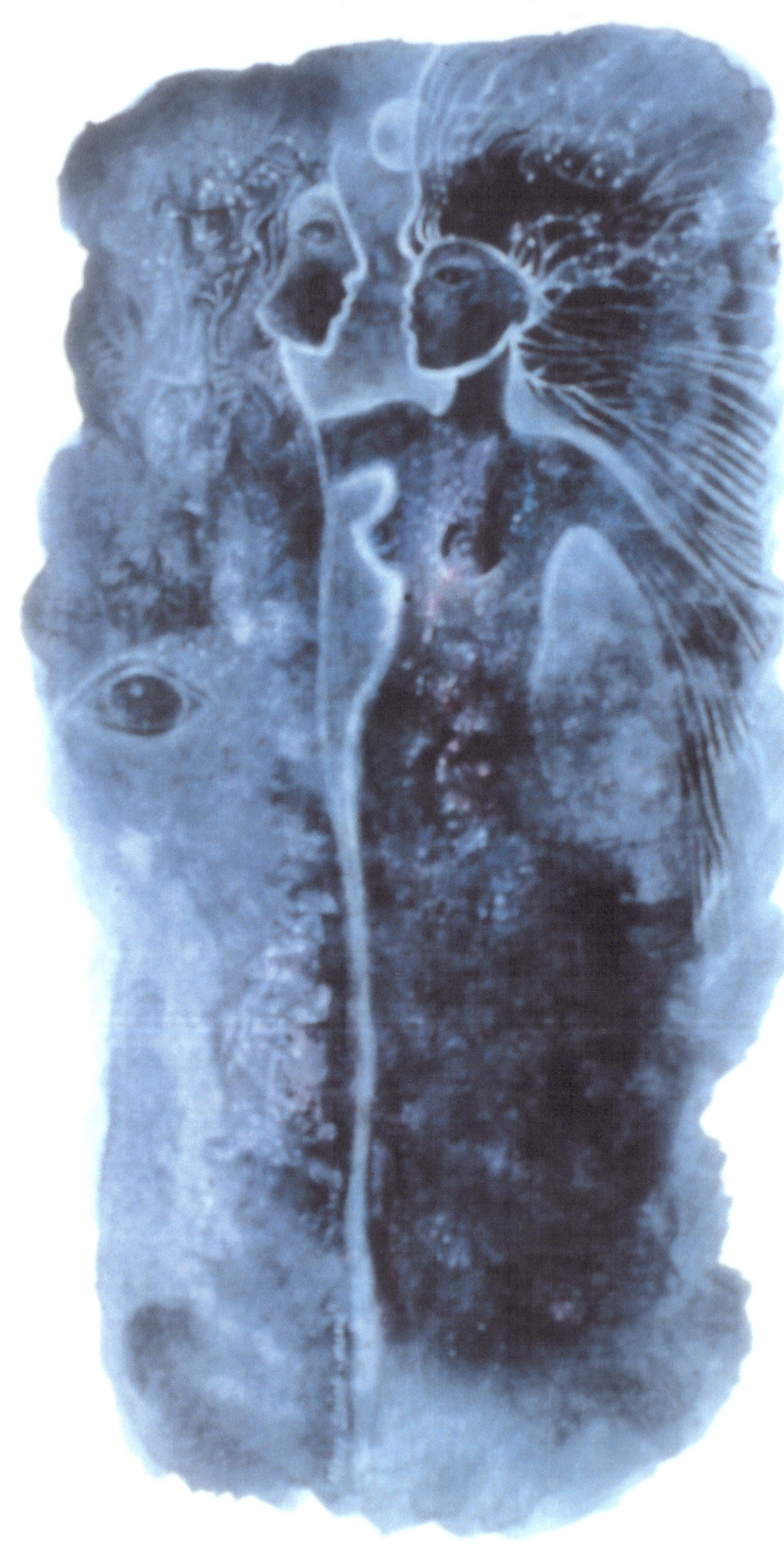

Changing Woman's Star-Dance

naked...
this primal dance
of stars...
moves through fields
of light...

Changing Woman and He
...in this image...
are the living revelation
of the shapeshifting Archetype
that is Changing Woman.
Together...as One...
they overcome the seeming
boundaries of the formed
universe...

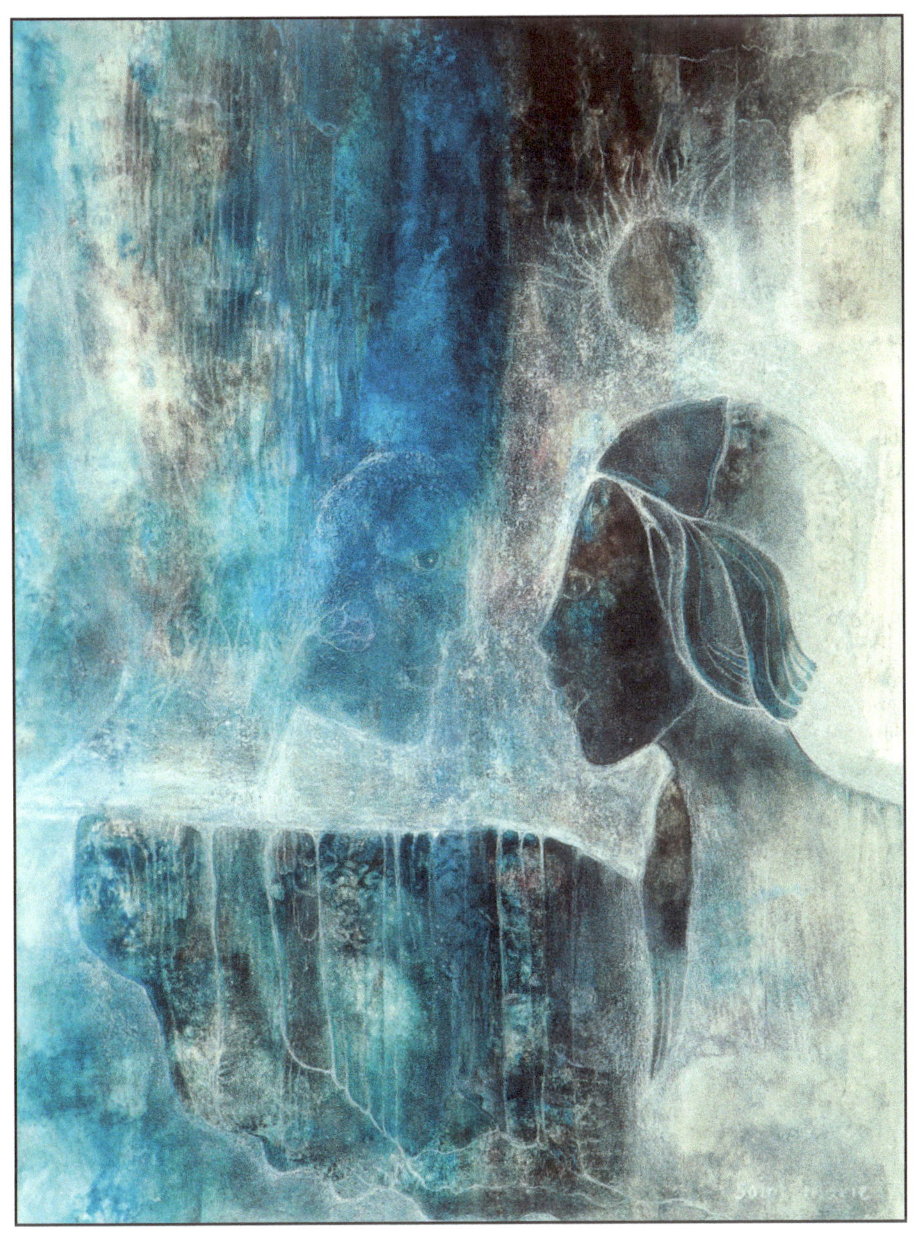

The Dance...of Beauty-SHE...

The Dance...of Beauty-SHE...
and all the fairy tales are true...

The Dance...of once upon a time...
to enter once again...the non-time...
paradox though it be...

And happiness...ever after...

This dance mirrors forth the opening of the grand containers that are the fairy tales. Contained in them are the gems to light the way...to the return to the One...that already Is...

Ancient Beauty HE and SHE

mystic union...filling all eternity...
leaving sounds of sorrow...
fleeing pain borne of past...

illumined countenance speaks...
...of worlds unseen...
...and ancient beauty Is...

Seen here is the outpicturing of the yin and yang of the universe in perfect equality and balance. Here in the union of the love and wisdom aspects of true man and true woman is born Beauty...

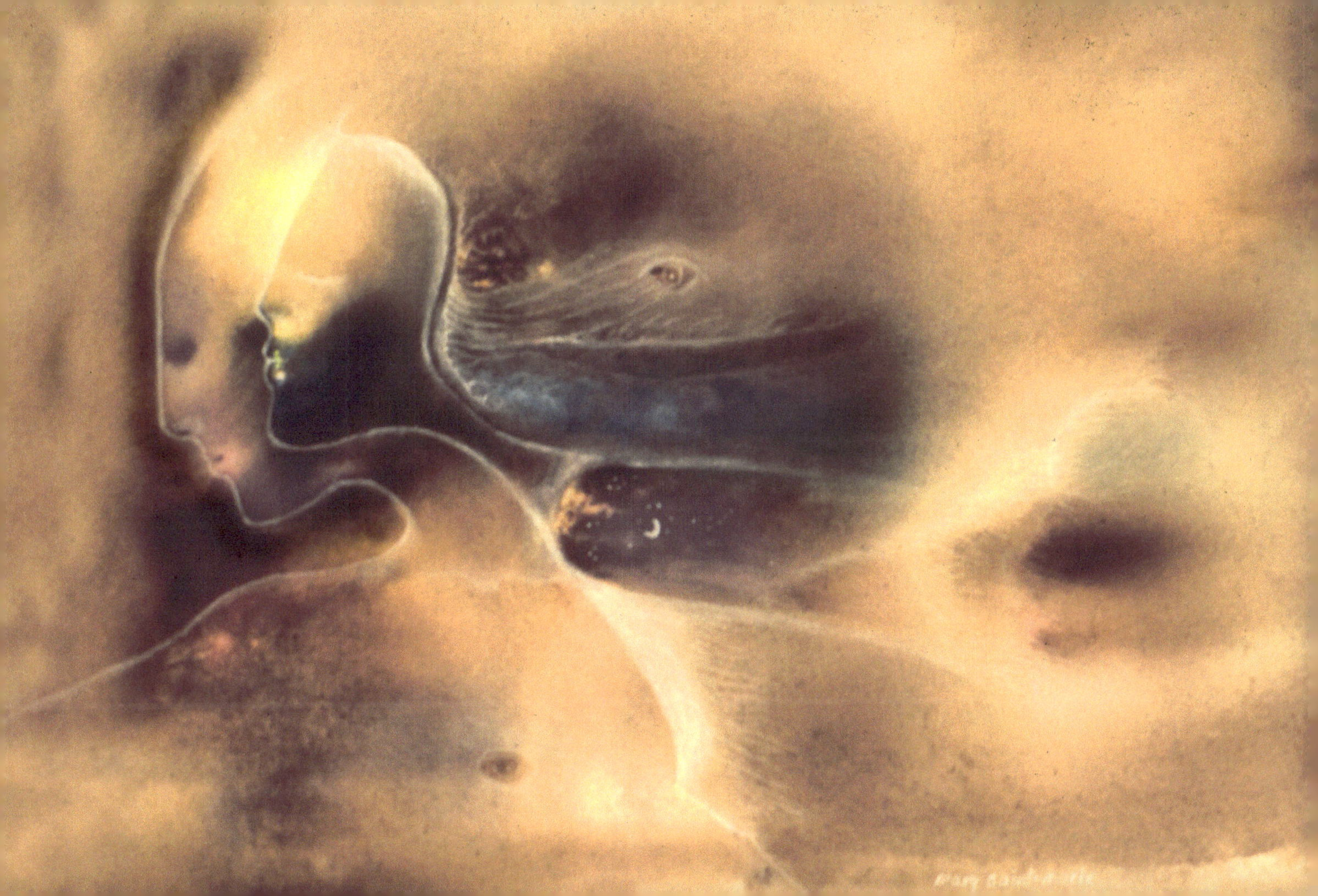

Robed HE and SHE

Robed dance among the stars...
does to Venus call...
Golden flowers and bees
do sing of an unknown world...
This world is come...
in flawless alchemy...
of bees...
drinking Venus
from the flowers...

This painting is an ode to the bees and flowers in their sacred roles in the evolution of humanity to the heightened Consciousness of Oneness. As such, Venus...SHE...does rule the very earth and the very sky... and balance...it is known.

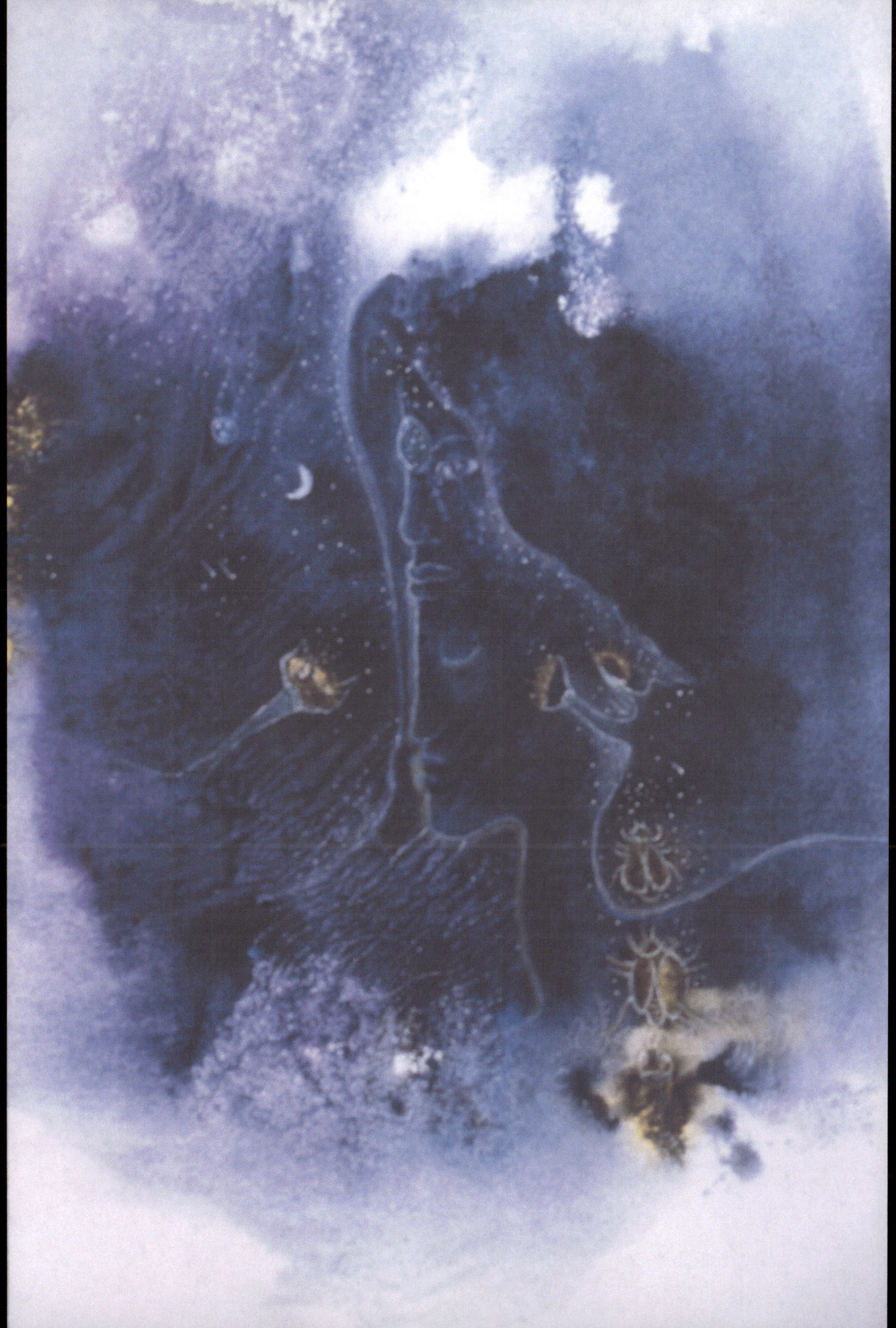

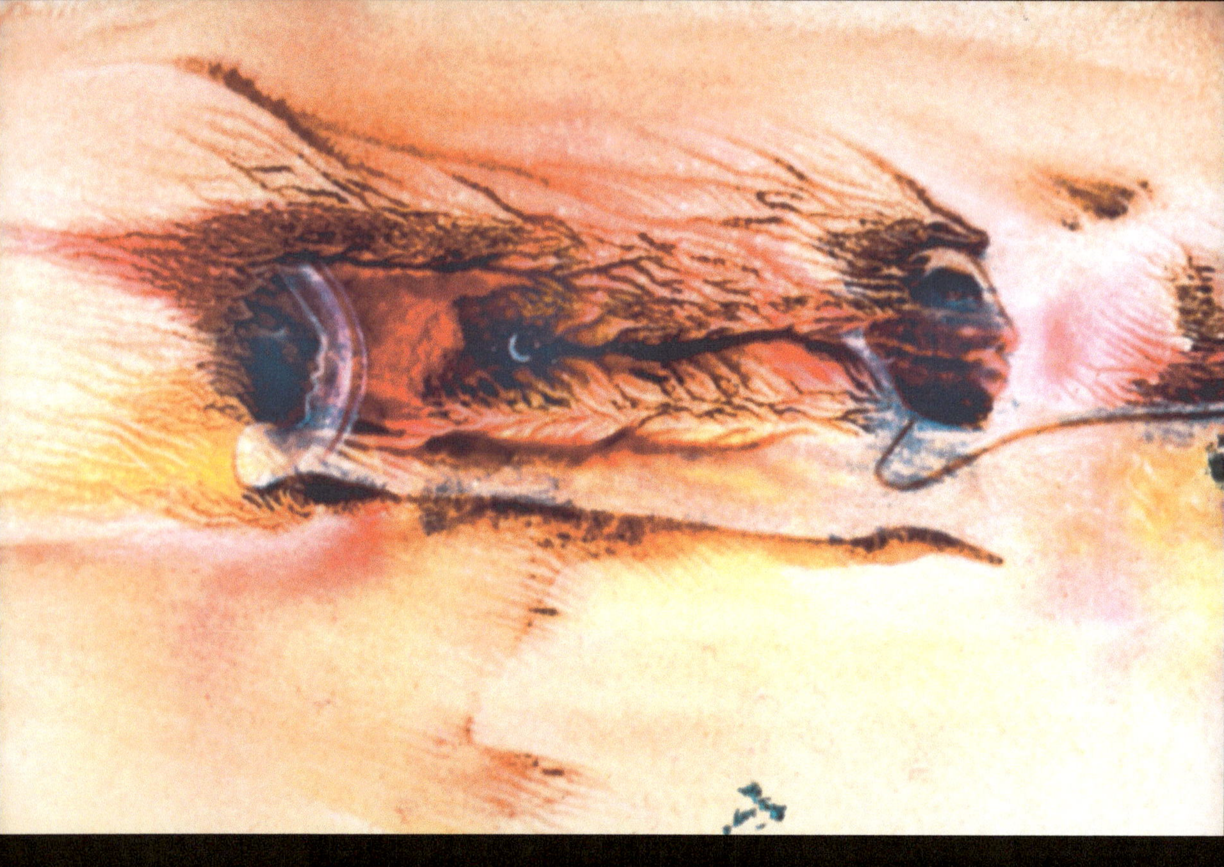

Mating Dance of The Sacred Two

together…do they dance…
…knowing both night and day…

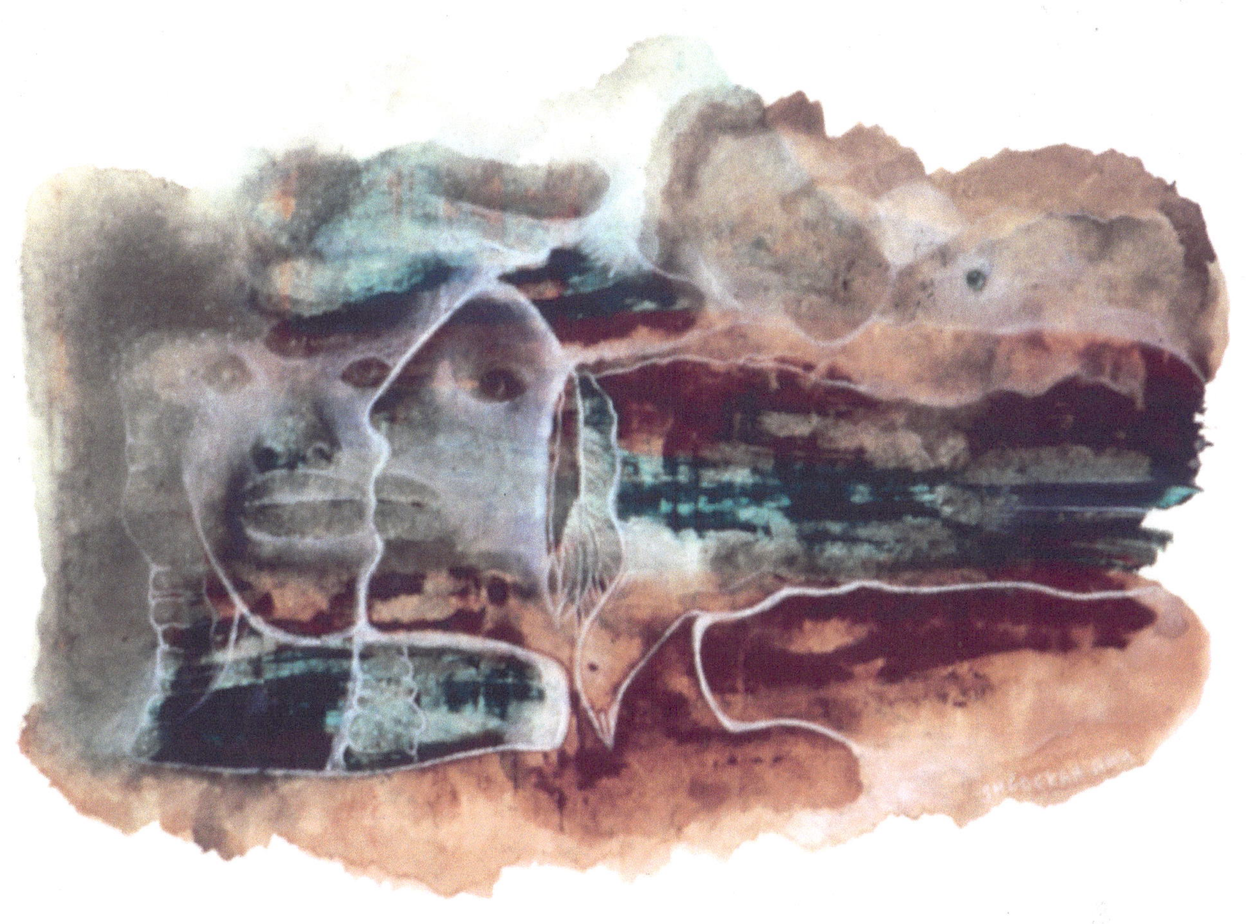

The Bird-Tribe Two

Incorporeal are they...
yet made of earth...
coming as two...
while they are one...

Felt here...is the peace of Archetypal HE and SHE...
They come as the embodiment of union...
while dressed they are in earth's attire...disguised in flesh and flowing raiment...

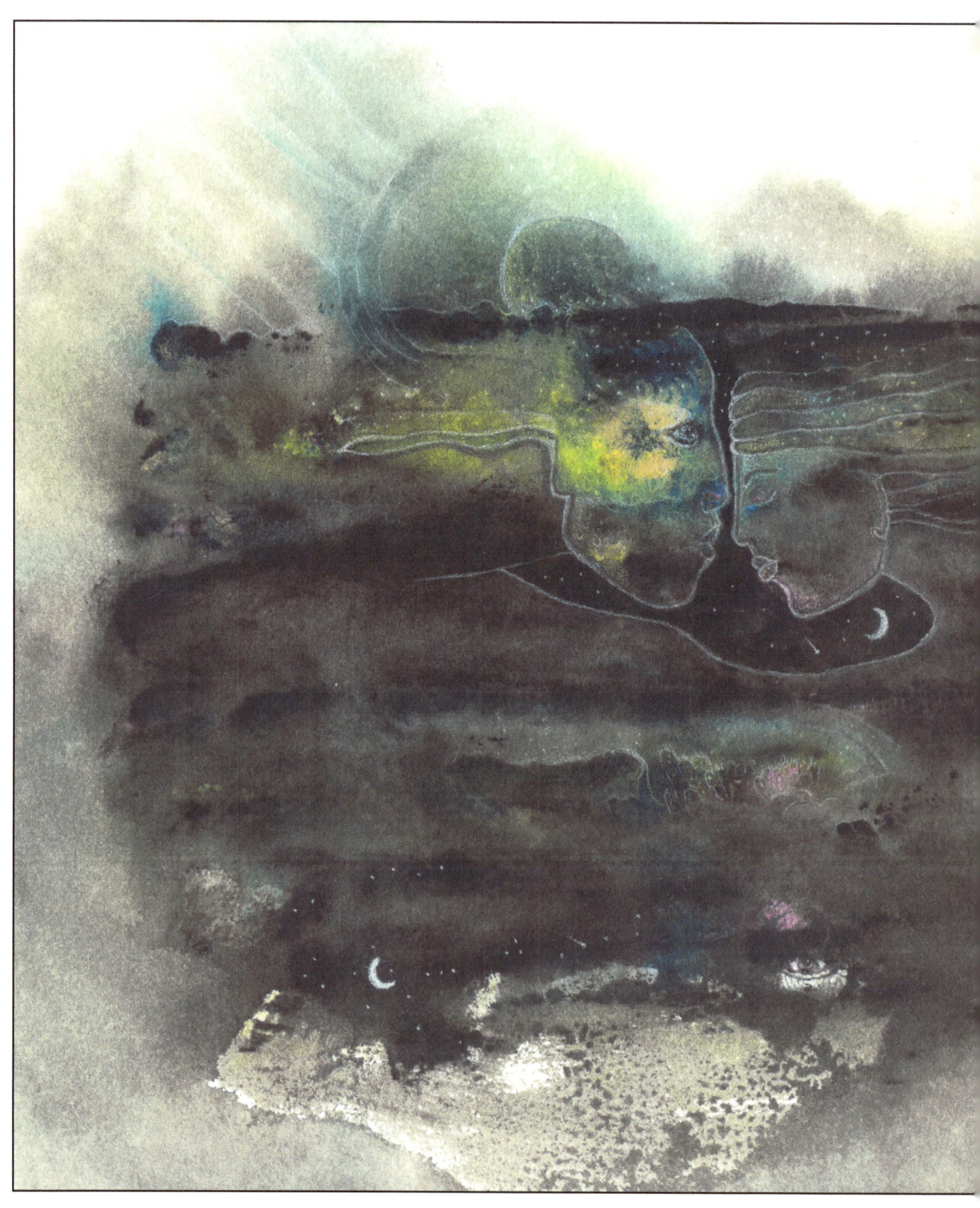

Marriage in the Kingdom

SHE and HE…in the Kingdom…
do find the shining jewels…

Together…they plant the flower…
the earth does smile their name…

This painting speaks
of the unspeakable rainbow marriage…
the joining together
of man and woman…
appointed by Grace…
the rare gem…
in a world which has forgotten.

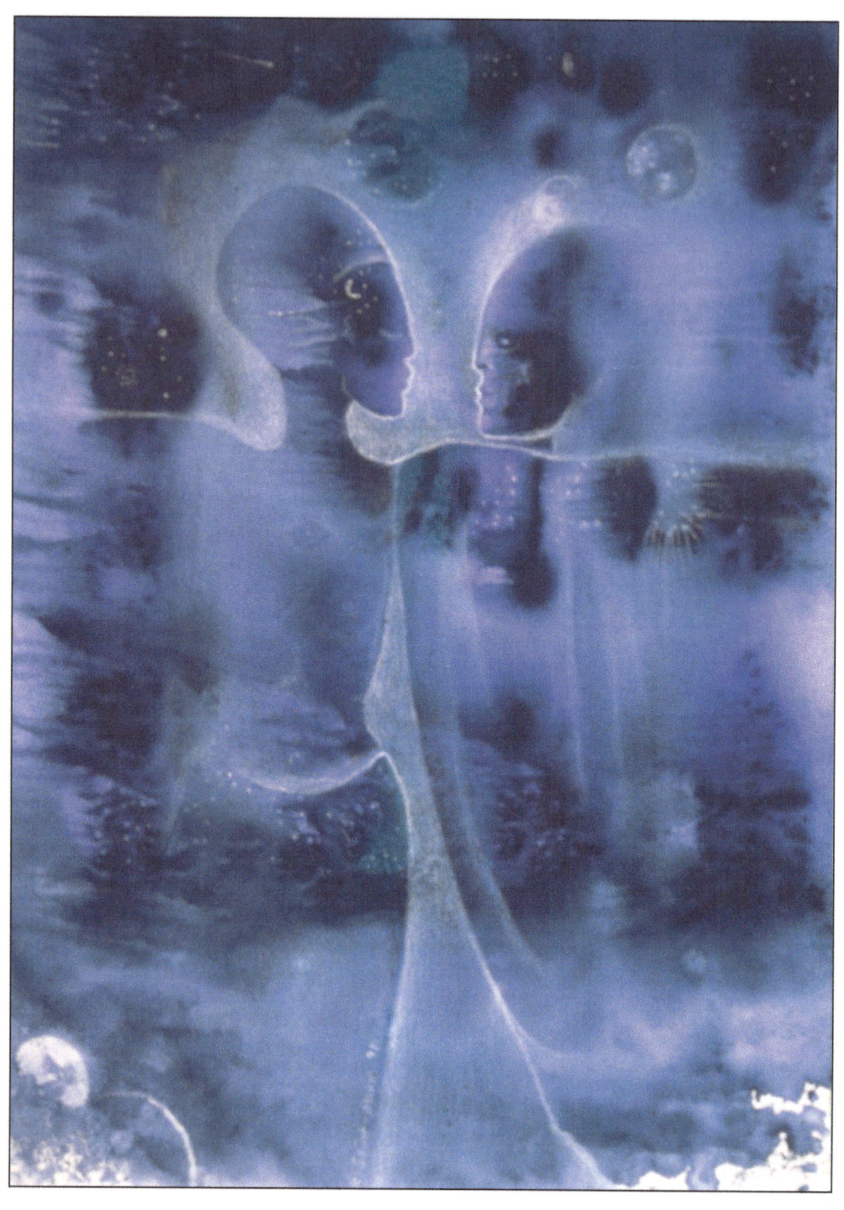

Star Woman-SHE and HE...
of the sacred dance...

o children of the world...
unearth yourselves...

diamond universes...wait...
unexplored by eyes...

the sacred dance is near...

This image inspires awareness of other starry realms.
Dance of man and woman is elevated to a consciousness of mystery and sacred alchemy.

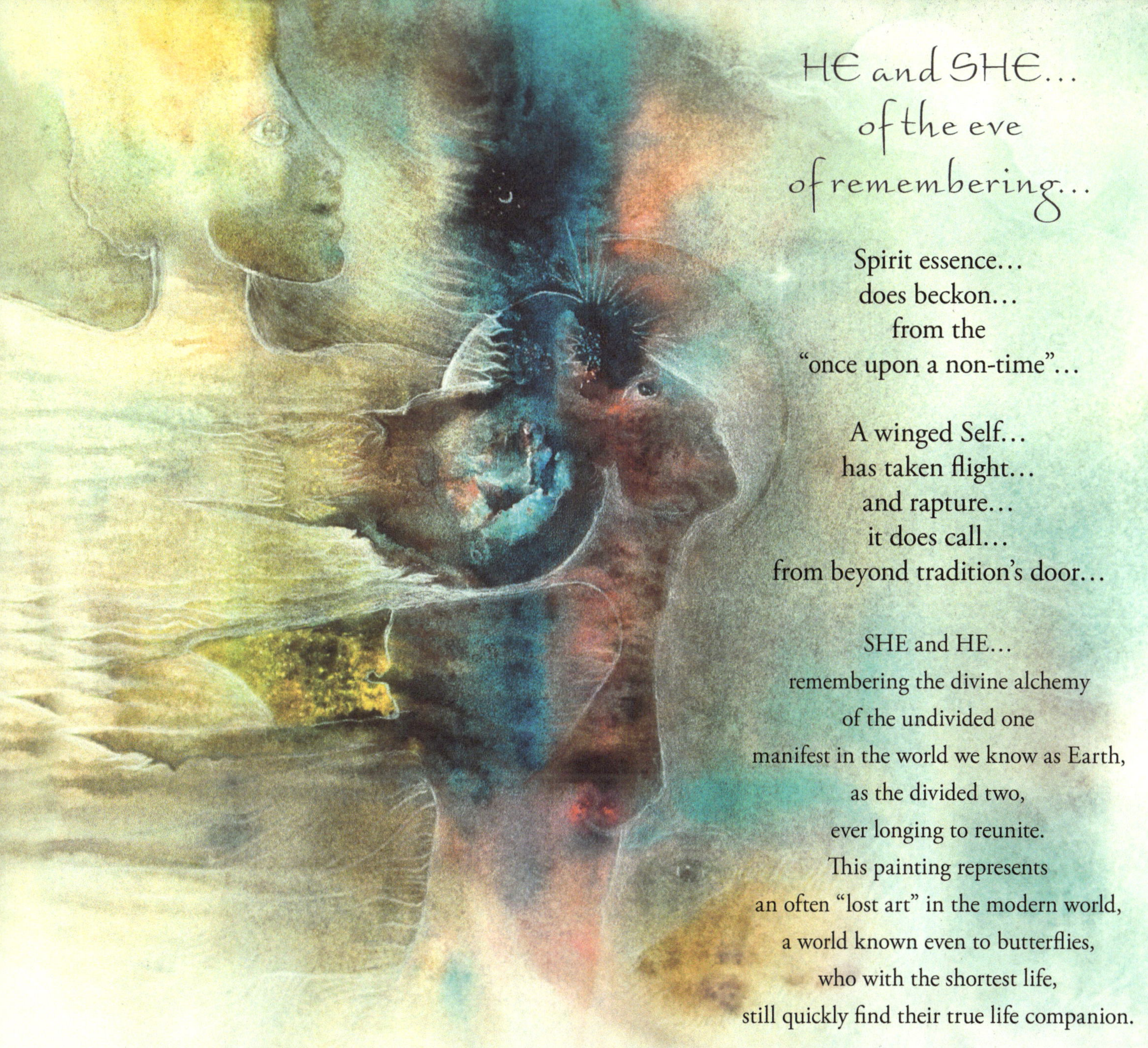

HE and SHE... of the eve of remembering...

Spirit essence...
does beckon...
from the
"once upon a non-time"...

A winged Self...
has taken flight...
and rapture...
it does call...
from beyond tradition's door...

SHE and HE...
remembering the divine alchemy
of the undivided one
manifest in the world we know as Earth,
as the divided two,
ever longing to reunite.
This painting represents
an often "lost art" in the modern world,
a world known even to butterflies,
who with the shortest life,
still quickly find their true life companion.

The Fool...at the edge

clothed in stars...
HE does wear the hat of fool...
for HE is everywhere...is everything...
and nothing at all...

This painting sings to us from past the stars...
It heralds The Fool...the Infinite...in form...

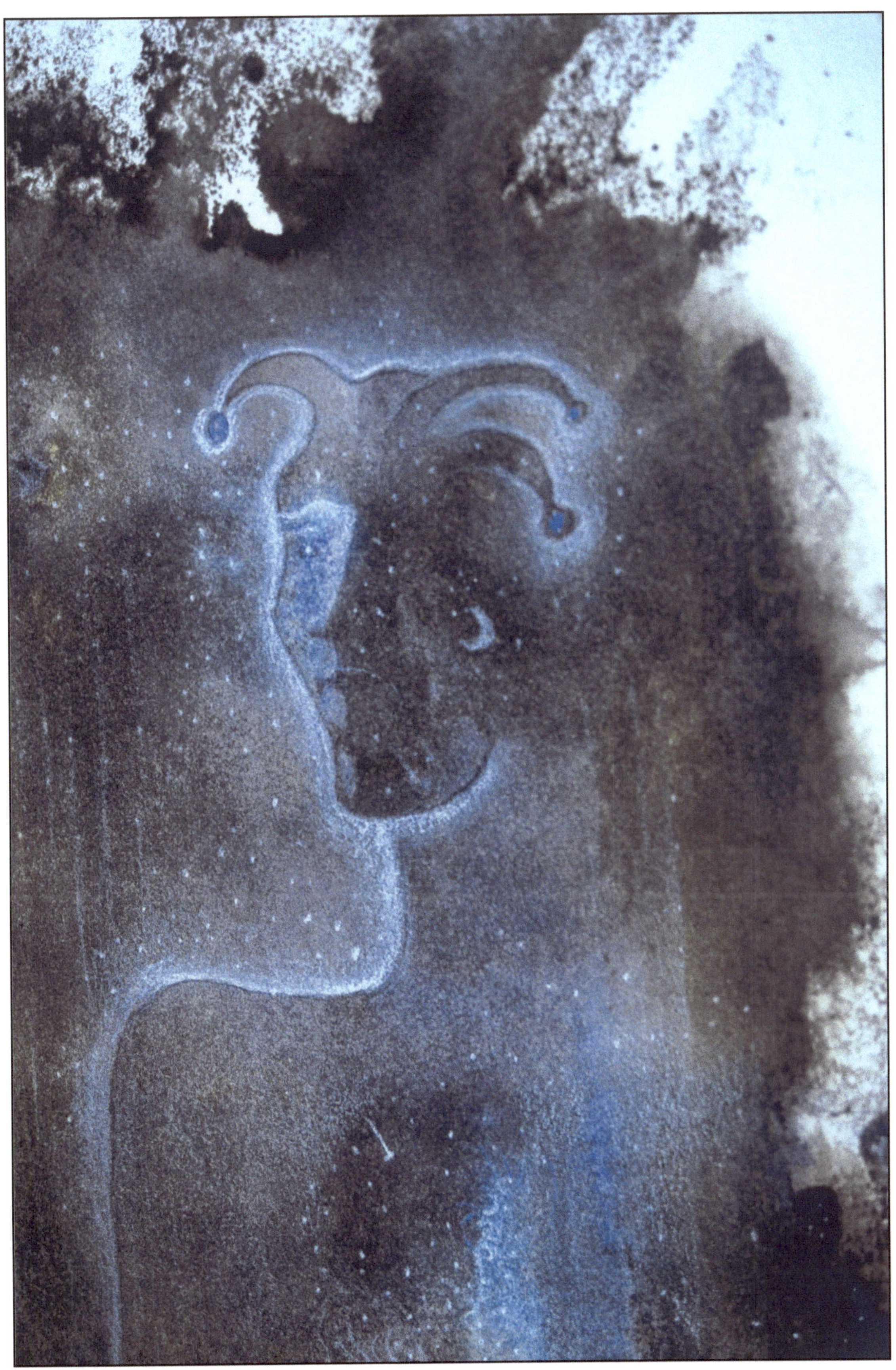

Poetry
of SHE and HE

I suckle a million breasts...

with no love...there is no tomorrow...
with no love...there is not hope...
with no love...the promise ends...

and so...my friends...
rise up...

rise up...
and find your way...

find the way...
in each other's smiles...
in your hugs...
and in no goodbyes...

I am borne each day within your hearts...
upon every kiss...
and in the wind...across the hills...

spare no moment...in finding me thus...
I am everywhere seen...
upon the lips of your dying...
in the throats of singers on stage...
in fashion gowns I walk...
and naked in the tribe...

I chant...
I sit amidst a stream...
I walk along the city streets...
I camp along faraway shores...

I sit in the sky...as a million stars...
I suckle a million breasts...
I stand in line in the markets of Earth...
I sing in the air as the rain...

I open your hearts in a million ways…
I caress you…
and open your doors…

hidden am I…
yet appearing with unceasing wonder…
a paradox in time…
I travel about…
to open all hearts…

enchanted am I…
in our home of earth…
of clay…of dust…of soil…
enchanted to find…
our marriage at last…
born in the hearts of smiling ones…
born in the hearts of love…

Caress Me

Live through me o great love…
Caress me…
Caress me in these morning hours…
And you shall see my smile…
My eyes do soften…
They gaze at nothing in particular…
Yet see Beauty everywhere…

O this love…does change my days
and it does change my nights…
No thing can tempt me from your arms…
Your embrace is all I need…
I will find my way in the days of your caress…

You are the suitor…which I have sought…
never in my reach…
You smile at me through every tree…
You touch me…when I breathe…

Caress me great love…
And let us arrive…at the wedding made for us…

The Call for Union

Paired by the Eternal…
two swans do share the mystery…
We've come…they say…
to tell you…
we are…pairs of forever…
we are…the call for union…

Unveiling of the Beloved

The Mystery…It Is…
and It comes…
It comes in the night…
unveils Itself…
and It dances…

Naked It stands…
waiting to be seen…
known only to holy sight…
union of HE and SHE…
known as the One…

Together…they return to the Beloved…
The Unknown…now known…
The Mystery…It Is…

Dance of the Wild Dakini

Through the doorway to the beloved…
is the dance of the wild dakini…

Atop mesas and mountains…
SHE sings the song of HE…
Together they are One…
and
together they light the Earth…
that emerges…

Come see…the dawning of this new day…

I am the wedding day

child…I am your beloved…the one you call so much…
I am your lover…the one you do await…
I am the lover and beloved…
I am the wedding day…
I am the union…of the day and night…
I am the caller and the one who's called…
I am the viewer and the viewed…
for me there is no heaven and earth…
for me there is just here…
…Here I am…no where else exists…
except in a mind that has no truth..

Let it be known that you are mine alone…
You are the One that I did choose…
Each known moment of your life…
shall enter from the mystery…
Your trust is mine…
and we do celebrate…
Your smile spreads across your face…
and light does glint across your eyes…

Wedded…we do walk and play
in joy upon the lands…
Wedded…do we see eternal shores…
and lightly step upon earth's sands…
Wedded…we are one through out the world…
with all who come our way…
Wedded…we shall explore the universe…
bringing truth to all who will…

Yellow flower and SHE

SHE…it is…who heralds…
a new way…
SHE…it is…who prays…
near the flower…
SHE…it is…who remembers…
times gone by….
SHE…heralds the garden…

This painting appears to be a mystical landscape.
It is calling into memory our oneness with the precious flowers and all that is.
Out of the Silence this memory takes flight into our world.

Some would think this imagination and dreamscape…
when truly it is Realism seen from a higher altitude.
It is the place…where Reality is felt, experienced, realized.

Friends…we must feel to create a different world...

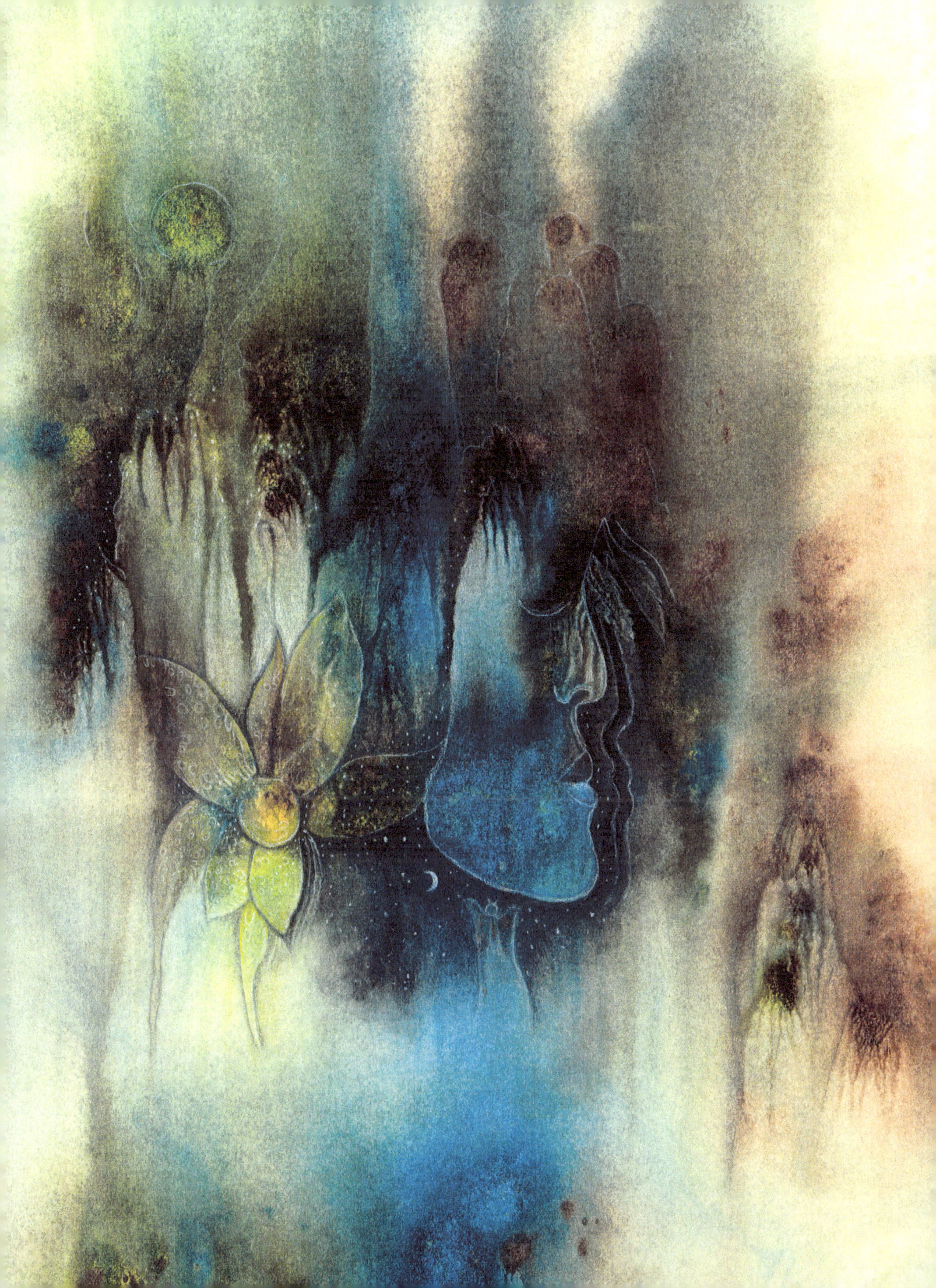

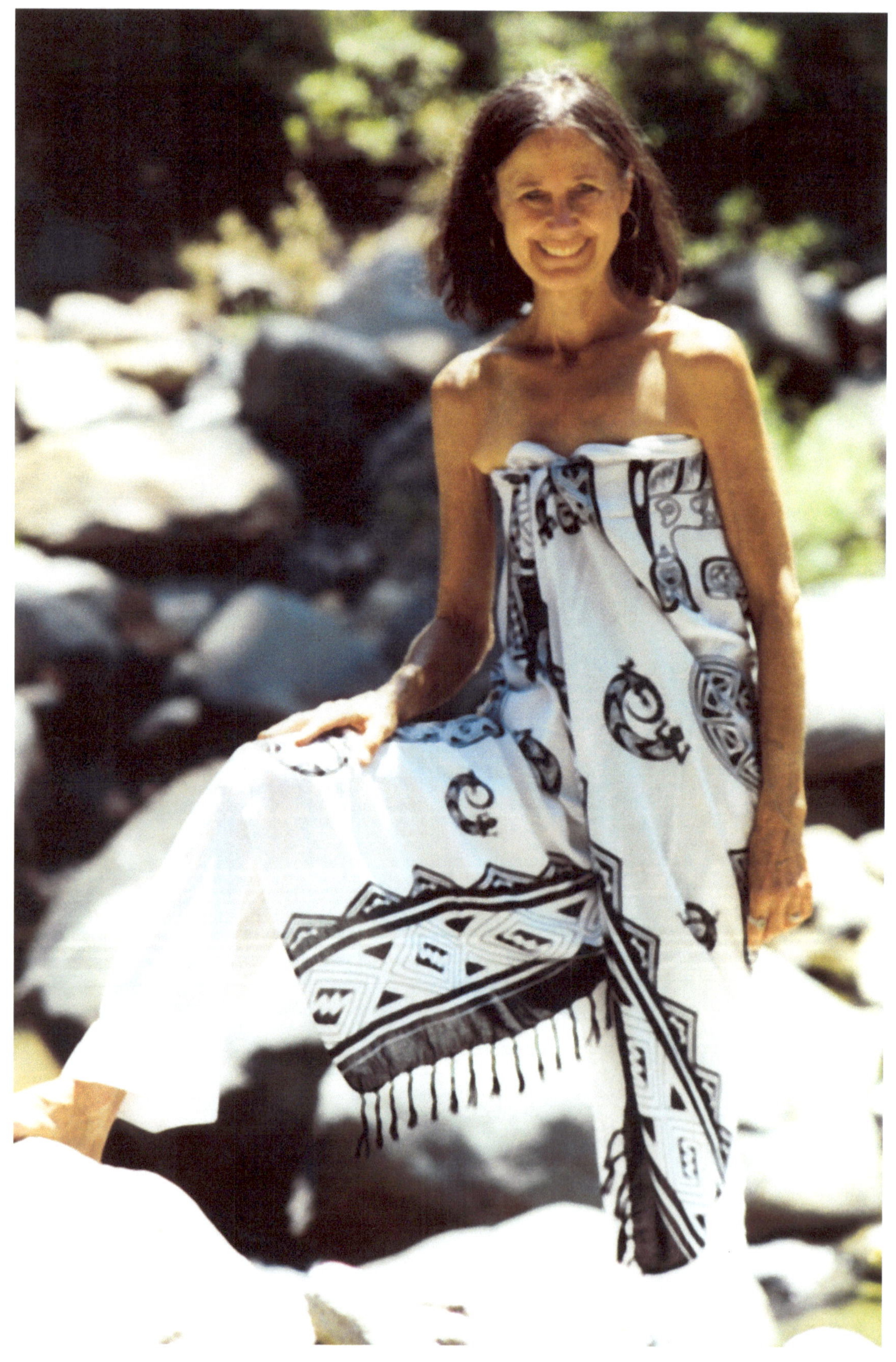

About the Artist-Writer

Mary Saint-Marie is a mystic artist, writer, poet, sculptress, and spiritual educator. *The Sacred Two* follows four previous books, *Galactic Shamanism, The Holy Sight, Nectar of Woman,* and *Messages from the Silence.* More recently, Mary has written a play, *The Monitor and Laughter of the Gods,* which is now available in book form. The play was performed as sacred theatre in the well-known theatre destination, Ashland, Oregon. Other recent books are *The Star-Stone Ones, The Animating Presence,* and *The Oracle and the Dreamer.* The oracle book of New Earth parables serves as "life passages" from personal human consciousness to Consciousness. They gently guide others through a passage into "the garden that already is." They offer a mystical reception into the new emerging culture in great simplicity.

Journey of Consiousness, a meditation CD by Mary, guides ones through four shifts of consciousness to the higher Consciousness, I Am Awareness. Mary also has two recordings, *She…it is…who Remembers* and *Return to Oneness.*

Mary has traveled extensively with her visionary art exhibits nationwide, with over one hundred and fifty showings. She has also traveled nationwide with Soul Sessions, workshops, and multi-media enactments inspiring others into the awareness of Oneness of the Sacred Presence, that each may come to express their true nature and essence. She describes the work as The Mystical as the Practical.

The visionary art of Mary Saint-Marie inspires and initiates. It mirrors our oneness with Creator and Creation. It is a reflection of the holy marriage of earth and sky. The yin and yang of all creation. It is a reflection of our true essence, our true identity as the one. It is an inner journey into the land of the Archetypal realms of wholeness. The paintings are witness to the Law of Balance, that is the law of love. The art gives voice to the Sacred. It is a visual offering of our transcendence. It is prayer…reminding us of the Undivided.

The Art-of-the-Soul paintings are multi-media, multi-technique, and multi-dimensional, ever unveiling the Unseen. The mixed media effects reveal a soul depth that is both primordial and galactic.

The visionary paintings and work are featured in *One Source Sacred Journeys, Songs from the Edge of Everything,* and *The Ways of Spirit.* The luminous body of work has appeared on cards, cds, books, calendars, and magazines, such as *Quest, Mystic Pop,*

Dream Network Journal, and *Anemone* in Japan. Mary's work has appeared on television nationwide on stations such as the Wisdom Channel, Bridging Heaven and Earth, Channel 5 in San Francisco. Mary's art was featured on television across Germany. Most recently, her art has been featured in the movie *FEMME,* a powerful film revealing the voice of the divine feminine through many women of the world.

The mystic art of Mary Saint-Marie is collected nationally and internationally in homes, offices, and retreat sites. Ever...it is an invitation inward, calling ones Home. Ever...it depicts and reminds us of our Christed Self. The One Self.

Mary has been pioneering visionary art exhibitions that reveal universal principles of Oneness since 1972 in galleries, conferences, symposiums, expositions, faires, workshops, and retreats. Her exhibit listing is available on request.

Note: Art collectors, buyers, and art lovers are invited to Mary's website and to her three art books. The books represent three separate phases of the artist's reflection of the Eternal, the I Am Awareness.

The books are: *The Sacred Two, The Star-Stones Ones,* and *Art As Consciousness..*

Biography and Education

Nature was the first potent childhood teacher of Mary Saint-Marie.

Barefoot was her life…running through deep gushing rain in the roadside ditches of Iowa and flying on great vines across ravines of Mississippi and riding great sea turtles on an island in the Gulf of Mexico.

And great was the inspiration of a pioneering pilot mother. Nature provided experiences of a wild oneness…that brought great joy of freedom…later to be captured in painting, writing, sculpting, dancing and sounding.

Formal university education included a degree in Education-English, after which she spent eight years teaching high school and college English, Mythology and Communication. She was also coordinator in public educational TV. Simultaneously Mary studied Fine Art at the University of Wisconsin.

Soon after this Mary had a spontaneous soul merging experience followed shortly by a head-on car collision that provided the opening to see her life *via her soul…as pure joy*. After this Mary could see emanation of light around living things. The exalted experience of the collision initiated a new life. Mary was inspired to begin her life as an artist and to make a solo journey 'overland', with a kelty pack filled with one change of clothing and art supplies on her back, to Spain, Morocco, Italy, Greece, Crete, Turkey, Iran, Afghanistan, Pakistan, India and Kashmir, where she felt the art, culture, heart and soul of those peoples.

Upon her return to the U.S., Mary began her first art exhibitions and pioneering shows for mystical and visionary art of the soul. She traveled to wilderness areas for nearly two years, once again feeling the oneness provided by Nature.

Beginning in 1974, Mary has lived mainly in a quiet mountain retreat in Mt. Shasta, California. She is the mother of two grown daughters.

Creative Process and Inner Journey

Mary Saint-Marie draws and paints from within, allowing herself to be a vessel for expressing art. She enters the emptiness before painting or sculpting...then meditates on the ONE...Light...Presence. Her mystical and sacred art of the soul reflects her experiences and journeys to the inner world of Spirit. Mary allows the ancient beauty of primordial, primal, archetypal imagery to reflect itself from the negative spaces of the mixed media, working in reverse. Mary works with *feeling the essence...the holy presence,* playing back and forth between the form and formless, the visible and invisible...always using the human form as the *temple template of Infinity,* and allowing it to reveal the *ethnic blends and bleed-throughs* from all time and space and from the timeless realm.

By meditating on the Oneness, the experience of the mergings and blendings with all the kingdoms and the elements of The Great Mother and with the divine archetypes may come. That we are One...may be shared.

It is then we glimpse our own 'Star-Stone Essence', our multi-dimensional nature...what I playfully call Galactic Shamanism...or the marriage of earth and sky...or more simply put... love, says Mary.

A note about the creative process as communication:

The multi-techniques and multi-media that have been used in this art for these visionary paintings heightens both the feeling of the galactic and the shamanic. The balance of earth and sky. The universal law of balance at play!

The unfinished and rough edges of the painting enhance the feeling of primal, primordial and shamanic. The Earth awareness is experienced. Shamanic.

The same edges may allow an elevated feeling of openness, of spaciousness. They allow the feeling of the Landing of Infinity (light manifestation) as the very Earth. The Invisible as the visible. Galactic.

Art, CDs, Soul Sessions, and Soul Retreats

www.MarySaintMarie.com
www.EarthCareGlobalTV.com

Art:

All art in Art as Consciousness is available as giclee fine art reproductions.

Inquire to find out if pieces are available as originals.

Please email to find the names of current gallery showings.

*See the website to view videos/YouTubes with art.

Books:

Galactic Shamanism
The Sacred Two
The Holy Sight
Nectar of Woman
Messages from the Silence
The Star-Stone Ones

The Animating Presence
The Monitor and Laughter of the Gods, a play in book form
Art As Consciousness
The Oracle and the Dreamer

CDs:

Journey of Consciousness, a meditation
Soul Sounds of World Birth

Recording:

Return to Oneness, a recording giving Voice to the Animals and addressing Rights of Animals (will be made available as a cd)

Soul Sessions and Retreats:

*Please see the website to find out more about the spiritual education for individuals and groups. Mary works both in person and by phone.

EarthCare Global TV

Please see the website for the full vision of a profound unification of Earth care (www.EarthCareGlobalTV.com).

EarthCare Global TV has as its purpose to freely educate and inspire people of the world about Earth care. It serves to unify ones of like vision through communication and Vision in Action.

EarthCare Global TV sees the understanding of the Universal Law of Balance in all of Nature being shared worldwide that the principle may be realized in daily life by all. The vision shares the practical understanding of the need of purity and sustainability.

*Please see the category, Internet TV, on the website, to see the listing of 270+ Earth care documentaries. The documentaries are about being a Voice for the Earth. And they are education and inspiration for humanity to choose a new direction: Purity instead of pollution.

*See also the category, Videos, on website to view youtubes about the Earth, created with the art of Mary Saint-Marie.

1. earth care, a short video created for The One Minute Shift, to expand awareness of the oneness of everyone, everything and everyplace.

2. *Holy Sight for the Earth and for the Sky*, an animation meditation

www.EarthCareGlobalTV.com

www.ingramcontent.com/pod-product-compliance
Lightning Source LLC
LaVergne TN
LVHW070122110826
845147LV00002B/173

* 9 7 8 0 9 6 4 6 5 7 2 8 1 *